Haunted Places
of
Derbyshire

Jill Armitage

COUNTRYSIDE BOOKS
NEWBURY, BERKSHIRE

First published 2005
© Jill Armitage 2005

COUNTRYSIDE BOOKS
3 Catherine Road
Newbury, Berkshire

To view our complete range of books,
please visit us at
www.countrysidebooks.co.uk

ISBN 1 85306 947 7
EAN 978 1 85306 947 5

Acknowledgements
I would like to give a big thank you to all the people who have contributed
stories and little-known facts that are included in this book; and to my
husband for his support, especially when the going got scary.

Cover illustration by Anthony Wallis

Designed by Peter Davies, Nautilus Design
Produced through MRM Associates Ltd., Reading
Typeset by Jean Cussons Typesetting, Diss, Norfolk
Printed by Arrowsmith, Bristol

·Contents·

• Introduction •

I was at my brother-in-law's bedside just before he died; so too was my husband, my niece Sue and my father-in-law, although the latter had been dead for eight years. Afterwards Sue said to me, 'I knew my father was going to die because Granddad had come to take him away. Didn't you see him sitting in the corner?'

Nurses will tell you similar stories of materialisation. At the old Royal Hospital in Chesterfield, two nurses working in the ward-office during the early hours of the morning heard voices and hurried into the ward to investigate. Around the end bed, they found a cloud of mist hovering but as they approached, the mist dispersed and they found the patient in the bed had died.

Some people refuse to leave until they are ready. Immediately after the death of a patient at Ashgate Hospital, their familiar and distinctive footsteps were heard walking away. Also a porter entering a morgue was shocked to see a man sitting on one of the two trolleys. The porter questioned why he was there, but the man grinned then appeared to float away, straight through a wall.

An elderly gentleman was taking his usual stroll along the public footpath that skirts the River Derwent, when ahead of him he saw an old friend. He intended to catch up and have a few words but first, he leaned down to pick up a broken tree branch and throw it in the river. As he straightened up he was amazed to see that the man had disappeared. He was so perturbed, he checked along the riverbank but found nothing and it was physically impossible for the man to have reached and mounted the stile in the next field in so short a time.

Hugely perplexed, when he later returned home, he was told that his old friend, the one he had just seen on the riverbank, had died that morning.

These apparitions are known as wraiths, spectral figures of living people, appearing some distance from their physical bodies. They are most likely to be seen by people who have a close relationship with the person, and reports of apparent bilocation are usually associated with imminent death.

Some holy people and occult adepts are believed to be able to perform such feats at will, but many more just appear to be grounded. One of the elderly residents of St Werburgh's House Nursing Home, Spondon, claims to have seen and spoken to a ghostly monk. This could, rather unkindly, be blamed on senile dementia but research shows he is just one of many to have witnessed this spectral visitor. The building used to be Spondon vicarage and when, in 1939, the Reverend Henry Cleeve Brocklehurst was very ill, a visiting parishioner saw the dying vicar deep in conversation with a monk.

So whether grounded or in visitation, this book is dedicated to the spirits that linger indefinitely. If you should meet one, please don't scream too loudly, you might frighten it away!

Jill Armitage

•North-west Derbyshire•

CHAPEL-EN-LE-FRITH

Chapel-en-le-Frith churchyard where a ghostly Scottish lament is heard.

According to a letter sent by Dr James Glegg, a non-conformist minister of Chapel-en-le-Frith, to his colleague the Revd Dr Ebenezer Latham, strange happenings took place at a church in Hayfield in August 1745. Strange is too bland a word to describe what several spectators witnessed in broad daylight; unbelievable would be more graphic.

Apparently in the churchyard was a large communal grave which suddenly opened to allow hundreds of unclad bodies to emerge and ascend quickly out of sight, singing in unison.

Dr Clegg's own town of Chapel-en-le-Frith has a less bizarre though more repugnant story relating to its graveyard, which is apparently the haunt of numerous Scottish ghosts. In September 1648, 1,500 Scottish Royalist soldiers, taken prisoner after the Battle of Ribble Moor, were herded south and crammed into the tiny church at Chapel-en-le-Frith. The doors were then closed and remained locked for sixteen days. In that hellhole, 44 men died on their feet and many more were very close to death. The dead were buried hastily in the churchyard.

Even though the 13th century church was later replaced, the churchyard is still there, and visitors who are unaware of the atrocity, claim to feel intense melancholy. Some have reported hearing the sound of groaning men, and one couple said they heard a Scottish lament being sung.

CASTLETON

Initially called Castle of the Peak, Peveril Castle stands in a dramatic hilltop position with magnificent views across the Hope Valley. It is one of the best-preserved Norman castles in Britain, its original purpose being to control the surrounding area, and in particular the lead mining interests in the High Peak.

The main tower or keep, built in 1155, was used as a vantage point, a last resort if the castle was stormed, and added greatly to the symbolic function of the castle, declaring its owner's power and status. Ironically it is the keep that is still so remarkably preserved today. It contains only one room on the entrance floor, and one basement room reached by a spiral staircase, that was probably used for storage.

It is in this basement room that English Heritage staff who work at the castle have had strange experiences.

Carol has regularly been aware of a presence, although she has never felt

Peveril Castle with its predominant keep, haunt of a monk.

threatened by it. In fact she talks to it and considers it to be quite friendly and calming. All the staff agree that they often feel they are not alone.

It would be nice to think that it's the ghost of an anomalous character known as Daft Sammy. Described as a shrewd lunatic, Sammy was a self-appointed castle guide several centuries ago, whose inexhaustible store of anecdotes and local knowledge did much to promote Castleton.

But Sammy is not alone. One visitor returned to the site gift-shop in such a state of agitation that staff were concerned. They thought he had over-exerted himself with the climb and wanted to call paramedics. Shaking his head, he informed them he was not ill, he had just seen a monk, as plain as day, by the side of the gatehouse, the remains of which stand at the top of the zigzag path. His distressed state confirmed he was not fabricating.

Other visitors have testified to seeing a white knight standing near the ramparts, a phantom dog and a horse, and some have reported the sound of an ethereal lady singing a soft lament from the sombre ruins. Even though the majority of visitors don't see or hear anything, most agree there is a definite atmosphere around Peveril Castle.

Sammy – the self-appointed guide to Peveril Castle.

The town of Castleton nestling at its feet was built in association with the castle, and was originally surrounded by a defensive bank and ditch. The zigzag path up from the town was literally the back entrance for the traders and craftspeople of Castleton who served the castle.

Like the castle, Castleton also has its share of ghosts. I spoke to a council workman who swore he had seen a cavalier riding down the main road one morning, a chamber-maid who couldn't close certain wardrobe doors until the ghost allowed her to, and staff at the Castle Hotel which boasts four resident ghosts.

My enquiries coincided with a visit by a team from Sky's Discovery Channel filming in the Castle Hotel and the graveyard, but would the ghosts of Castleton be party to this?

At the Castle Hotel, the team could encounter the jilted bride who walks along the corridor to the raftered dining room where her wedding breakfast was set many years ago. Or the lady dressed in grey could drift through, or the man in his mid fifties wearing a blue pinstriped suit. They may even glimpse the misty figure of a woman who appears to wade waist-deep in the floorboards.

The landlord who witnessed this later found out that the floor of the corridor where she had been seen, had been raised during construction work and the altered height meant that the spectre was in fact walking on the original floor level.

WINNATS PASS

In the 17th and 18th centuries, eloping couples made their way to Peak Forest, the Gretna Green of Derbyshire, where they could marry without prior notice or parental consent. One such couple was Clara and Alan, who in 1758 took the perilous journey from their native Scotland.

Reaching Castleton, they asked directions at an inn where they were watched by five burly miners who, guessing Clara's wealth from her attire, hatched a plan to relieve the young couple of their possessions.

Next morning Alan and Clara resumed their journey and began the steep climb out of Castleton through the hazardous limestone gorge, once a major route into the town and known as Wyndeyates, meaning the pass through which the wind sweeps. These days it is called Winnats Pass.

A period photograph, dated 1909 of Winnats Pass, where the ghosts of two young lovers can still be seen trying to escape by scrambling up the rocky sides of a cliff, hand in hand.

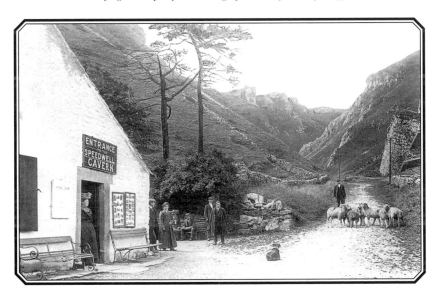

Clara became uneasy as they picked their way on horseback through the narrow gully flanked by looming walls of rock, and as they neared the centre of the pass, the five miners leapt from their hiding place and dragged the couple from their horses.

Alan put up a fight and Clara begged for mercy, but both were brutally axed to death. Their battered, lifeless bodies were flung down a mine and the men shared out the couple's £200. Later, when Clara and Alan's horses were found wandering near the pass, there was little doubt amongst the locals that something had happened to the young couple, but with no proof or bodies, no one was ever brought before the courts.

Then people began hearing strange noises coming from the centre of Winnats Pass. There were stories of blood-curdling screams, strange thudding sounds and the sudden appearance of a young couple who would then mysteriously disappear.

But in nemesis, the murdering miners did pay the price for their crime. Nicholas Cook died within a year, John Bradshaw and Francis Butley were killed by a mysterious rock fall in Winnats Pass, and Thomas Hall took his own life. The fifth man, James Ashton, persecuted by his crime, made a death-bed confession to the vicar of Castleton.

There is however, mute evidence of the crime now practically forgotten. Although in a poor state, Clara's side-saddle can be seen in a glass case amongst mining artefacts in the Speedwell Cavern Gift shop, at the entrance to Winnats Pass. This is only a short distance from the place where, it is said, on moonlit nights, the ghosts of the two young lovers can still be seen trying to escape by scrambling up the rocky sides of a cliff, hand in hand.

HATHERSAGE

Once labelled the most haunted house in Derbyshire, the story of Highlow Hall at Hathersage goes back to the days of 1340 when Nicholas Eyre, eldest son of the Lord of the Manor of Hope was a frequent visitor. The cad was having a relationship with both the Archer sisters,

Highlow Hall, haunted by the heiress.

the co-heiresses of the property. Not surprisingly, when the eldest sister caught him at his little game, she was not too pleased and what happened next we can only surmise, because she disappeared from Highlow in circumstances unknown.

The two-timing Nicholas Eyre married the younger daughter and would have lived happily ever after if her sister hadn't re-appeared as a ghost. This must have been rather awkward, because she not only blamed Nicholas Eyre for her death, she put a curse on the family. She said that the Eyre dynasty would prosper to the fifteenth generation, then they would dwindle into insignificance. The curse did in fact come true as the various branches of the family became extinct and the extensive acres dwindled.

Did the disappearance of the jilted sister have any connection with the bumps that are heard from time to time on the staircase treads? Legend says yes. They are said to be the phantom echoes of an incident when a lady was murdered in one of the upstairs bedrooms and her body dragged along the landing and down the stairs to be buried in an unmarked grave.

Heralded by a rustle of silk skirts, a ghostly lady was often seen crossing the old courtyard to enter the front door and ascend the oak staircase. She has also been seen standing with the palms of her hands resting on the edge of a cattle trough gazing into the water and no doubt contemplating her own reflection and wondering why Nicholas Eyre jilted her in favour of her sister.

ABNEY

A carter in his horse-drawn trap made a regular journey along the lonely lane from Leadmill to Abney and on various occasions a phantom figure would appear and take the horse's bridle to lead it for a short way. This did not unduly disturb the driver or spook the horse but the driver's dog would cower in the trap, its hair bristling with fear. One day however, when the phantom appeared, the driver was caught off guard and involuntarily raised his whip. Instantly his arm fell to his side, limp and useless, and he never recovered from his paralysis.

EYAM

They say that an incident experienced by one person could be a figment of an overactive imagination but when the same thing is experienced by many it's more than just a coincidence. This is obvious in the tale of the phantom cyclist.

The first incident on record concerns two men who were walking through Eyam Dale one morning when they had to leap hurriedly aside to avoid being run over by a cyclist racing down the steep gradient. Turning to curse the cyclist, the men were shocked to see that the road was completely deserted.

Down this same stretch of road one dark night, a man was walking home when he distinctly heard the swish of the rubber tyres and ringing of a bicycle bell. He turned to stare in the direction of the noise but the cyclist never materialised.

A man and his wife were walking along when they heard a cyclist approaching from behind. They instinctively stepped into the side to let it pass just as a Chesterfield service bus approached from the opposite direction. The bus rounded a bend and swept the road with its headlights but there was no sign of a cyclist.

None of these people actually saw the phantom cyclist, but a keen cyclist did as he laboriously climbed the Eyam Dale one very wet day. Dripping with water and making hard work of the ascent, the cyclist was amazed to see another cyclist effortlessly overtake him and pull away. Not only that, the phantom cyclist was bone dry despite the fact that it was pouring with rain.

*   *   *

Eyam has gone down in history as the plague village where in 1665, two thirds of the villagers died. With this kind of high mortality rate, it's not surprising that it has its fair share of ghostly tales to relate. At the cottage where the outbreak began, a pleasant-faced lady in a blue smock haunts the front bedroom. She watches the sleeping occupants before fading slowly away. At Mompesson's Well, where outsiders left goods for the villagers who paid with coins dropped in vinegar, the ghost of a little boy is said to stand, watching and waiting.

During those turbulent months, victims were buried around the area. The Hancock family of Riley have their own little cemetery and a blue lady has been seen tending their graves. In the churchyard is the impressive tomb of Catherine Mompesson, wife of the Reverend Mompesson. At the outbreak of the plague he persuaded all the villagers to remain within the village to stop the plague spreading, and despite being in poor health, Catherine stayed to support her husband. That support cost her her life, and Catherine Mompesson's ghost is said to haunt the rectory and to wander between there and the church, pausing near the 8th century Celtic cross.

In the dell for many years stood a lonely, ruined cottage. Rumour said that a malevolent ghost lurked around the crumbling ivy-clad hovel and those who witnessed it described an old woman dressed in the fashion of long ago – a short

The Miner's Arms, Eyam, reputedly the village's most haunted building.

bedgown, a coarse woollen and cotton petticoat, a mob cap and shiny buckled shoes. Locals tried to avoid the cottage at all cost, yet this ghostly old dame didn't seem to be grounded to that particular spot. On bright moonlit nights, she was often seen scurrying across the dell at great speed, and entering neighbouring cottages to torment the terrified occupants as she pummelled and pinched their defenceless bodies. At one time she was known to tear the bedclothes off the horrified inhabitants. Strong doors and locks were no barrier to this spirit as she was seen on many occasions to enter a house as a puff of smoke through the keyhole or small cracks in walls.

The Miner's Arms has the title of the village's most haunted building, and it has a plaque to prove it. That's no mean acclaim in a village where almost every cottage had a resident ghost. During the 17th century, a former landlady died after being thrown down the stairs, and her ghost, dressed in an old-fashioned peaked bonnet and cape, is now said to wander round looking rather perplexed. Running footsteps have been heard upstairs and there have been strange occurrences in the bedrooms, possibly the most bizarre being the manifestation of some old medical equipment which appeared one night, but had gone by morning.

CALVER AND HOLMSFIELD

Not all ghosts are perceived to be human. There are many reports of ghostly animals, the most frequently reported being the dog.

A young woman was travelling between Calver and Calver Bridge late one night. It was dark and she felt frightened until she realised that she had the company of a large white dog. Although usually afraid of dogs, she found this one friendly and comforting. The dog stayed by her side until the lights of houses were reached, when it went its own way, disconcertingly disappearing through a solid stone wall.

Along the road from Calver Sough to Stoney Middleton, a Methodist minister was walking one night when he realised he was being followed. He was carrying the collection money from the various chapels he served and he felt rather vulnerable until he was unexpectedly joined by a large dog that stayed protectively by his heels until he reached his destination. Reaching down to pat the dog, his hand passed straight through it.

Ghost dogs vary in size, shape and colour and many, like the two examples above, are protective. Unfortunately they are not all. Not too far from Calver is the widespread village of Holmsfield. It lies almost on the Derbyshire/Yorkshire border, just a stone's throw from the sprawling Sheffield suburb of Totley. Holmsfield has tales of a ghostly black dog with huge staring eyes and backward pointing feet that roams the area.

Known as the devil's dog, or the Padfoot in the North of England, a black dog is said to presage tragedy if you are unfortunate enough to encounter it. Many folk in the Peak and surrounding district believed in the Rach Hound or Gabriel's Ghost Hound. Although never seen, these ghostly hounds were reputedly always heard yelping just before a death.

GRINDLEFORD

In a bluebell wood high above the River Derwent near Grindleford is an impressive stone statue. It would be in keeping in the garden of one of our stately homes, but here it is surrounded by rhododendron bushes and rowan trees and few can admire its beauty. Judging from the flowers she holds in her left arm, this is a statue of Flora, the Roman goddess of flowers, and many years ago, J. Castle Hall wrote a ballad entitled *The Astrologer's Daughter* linking this statue with a story.

Flora was a kind and beautiful girl and the daughter of a much-feared Gypsy astrologer. She had met and married a young man called Victor and they set up home together in a small cottage near Grindleford close to the woods where they had met. For a time they were extremely happy, then Victor had to go away to war.

The statue of Flora erected by a grieving husband in memory of the young lady who haunts the area.

Twelve months passed and Victor returned home to find the cottage abandoned. He was mystified and, as he stumbled through the woods on his way to find the answer, he saw his wife coming towards him, her arms outstretched. She was dressed in the purest white attire, but as he ran to embrace her, his arms passed through her outline as if it was a shadow. He had seen her ghost.

Apparently after he had left, Flora had died giving birth to a baby daughter. Victor never married again and in memory of his lost love, he erected the statue of Flora in an ancient grove, but her ghost is said to haunt the area still.

BUXTON

Buxton is Derbyshire's most famous spa town and the highest market town in Britain. According to a book entitled *Into an Hour Glass* by Nancy Price published by Museum Press, Buxton is also the haunt of at least five ghosts. Nancy Price was a celebrated actress, theatre manager and author who first went on the stage at Buxton as part of the Benson Company, and she wrote of her own ghostly experience when she and a friend found very reasonably priced rooms in a large house at Burbage, Buxton. It was comfortable and clean but had no electricity in the bedrooms.

On the first night, Nancy woke with a start, feeling there was someone in the room. Groping for the matches she lit a candle and woke her friend in the next room for reassurance. The next day neither of them said anything about the incident and by bedtime, Nancy had convinced herself it must have been indigestion and went to bed as usual.

Again she woke suddenly and distinctly felt something gripping her throat, but when her friend rushed in with a candle nothing could be seen. The following night they slept with the communicating door open, but this time, not only did Nancy feel fingers gripping her throat, she heard a voice whisper 'Remember!'

When questioned, the landlady broke down and admitted that, over 100 years before, it was reported that a woman and her lover had been pursued by a jealous husband who murdered them in that room.

*   *   *

One winter night, a man from Fairfield, Buxton, visited a farm three miles away. During his visit, there was a severe snowstorm and the man had to spend the night on the couch in the parlour. He was comfortable enough, yet he kept being disturbed by the loud whining of a dog in the room. Next morning, the guest told the farmer about the noisy dog, but the farmer declared that there was none. What he had heard was the spectre of their favourite dog, which had died three years previously.

ASHFORD-IN-THE-WATER

Lying in isolation one mile from Ashford-in-the-Water on the road from Monsall Head, this 19th century burial plot is like a roadside oasis surrounded by flat fields. Edged with mature trees and a stone wall, this is Infidel's Cemetery, so named because the gravestones apparently have no reference to God. I was unable to verify this as the rampant vegetation has almost swallowed them up. The plot is enclosed by a stone wall, and where that is broken, there is a substantial fence.

It was once thought to be the burial place of evil people which has compounded its reputation for being haunted by a vampire, a grey lady seen at dusk amongst the gravestones and a man in black who is seen outside the entrance and then disconcertingly vanishes through the wall.

GREAT LONGSTONE

Thornbridge Hall, now a private residence after years as a teacher training college, is situated on Shady Lane, Great Longstone. This is a stretch of country road, that runs between Great Longstone and Ashford-in-the-Water, and is overhung by mature trees. It is never very busy, but supposedly if you travel along there at dusk or dawn you are likely to encounter twelve men carrying a coffin. If you look closer, you will see that the men are headless and the coffin is empty. It is apparently intended for the unfortunate person who meets this strange funeral cortege.

HADDON HALL

The paranormal activity of Haddon Hall is neither well documented nor encouraged, yet there is definitely something that even the sceptics can't fail to notice. One visitor apparently witnessed a spectral cook in the kitchen beating a young kitchen lad, and another visitor said that her

The gardens of Haddon Hall.

twelve-year-old grandson who had accompanied her on a visit, felt so oppressed by presences, he simply couldn't walk through the long gallery. Members of staff have frequently heard footsteps in various places in the empty hall, and the head steward has experienced a presence while she was locking up. An ex-comptroller heard female voices and laughter in the courtyard, and there have been reports of music coming from the old Vernon Chapel.

But the most amazing experience happened to one of the staff about 20 years ago. He had just walked through the banqueting hall and started to climb the dog-leg stairs to the Long Gallery when he stopped in mid-stride. There, ahead of him at the top of the stairs was a woman in a dark Elizabethan dress. Yet she was no living, breathing woman, this was a fully-formed ghost.

As he stood transfixed, she rolled a gobbet of phlegm round in her mouth and spat it onto the floor, a habit we now find quite disgusting but which would have been quite acceptable in Elizabethan society. Taking a few seconds to compose

*The death mask of
Lady Grace Manners.*

himself, the man turned and ran. The experience had left him very shaken and he retired shortly afterwards.

On my many visits to Haddon Hall, I am always drawn to the death mask of Lady Grace Manners in the small museum. Lady Manners was the founder of the school in Bakewell which bears her name, and was the daughter-in-law of Dorothy Vernon, the eloping heiress. After psychometrising, I feel that it is this Lady Manners who is often in visitation at the Hall, and the probable spitting spectre.

BASLOW

One day, a tramp called at a thatched cottage in Baslow begging for food and, although she was cooking bacon for herself at the time, the lady of the house told him she had no food for lazy ruffians like himself. This so incensed the tramp that he forced his way inside, grabbed the pan and poured the boiling fat down her throat, scalding her to death.

Following his arrest and trial, he was sentenced to be hung in chains from a gibbet erected on Gibbet Moor just off the main Baslow/Chesterfield road, to die a slow and painful death. His screams were said to have so upset the Duke of Devonshire at Chatsworth House directly west of Gibbet Moor, that he brought about the legislation to prohibit such an inhuman practice.

This unknown tramp was the last person in England to be gibbeted alive and the poor man's screams are still heard. In July 1992 Jane Townsend reported

The thatched cottage at Baslow where the tramp murdered the householder.

hearing what she described as blood-curdling and petrifying screams while hiking in the area of Gibbet Moor.

But this is a double haunting. The cottage at Baslow is also said to be haunted by the murdered woman. According to the late Edgar Osbourne, a retired librarian and archivist at Chatsworth House who lived in the cottage, during times of illness when he was in much pain, the old woman appeared at his bedside and soothed him. Poor recompense for the way she refused the tramp!

CHATSWORTH HOUSE

Chatsworth House, seat of the Duke of Devonshire, is one of England's most famous stately homes. Every year, hundreds of thousands of visitors admire this unique and quintessentially English country house which has been open to sight-seers ever since it was built.

A water-colour of Chatsworth House 1828.

The first house at Chatsworth, begun in 1552, was built by Bess of Hardwick and her second husband Sir William Cavendish. After Sir William's death in 1557, Bess's third husband Sir William St Loe paid for the completion of the building, but he died in 1565. Two years later she married George Talbot, 6th Earl of Shrewsbury, but the marriage had problems and Bess moved back to her old childhood home at Hardwick.

Possibly the biggest problem was Mary, Queen of Scots. Queen Elizabeth I appointed the Shrewsburys her custodians, giving them the responsibility of keeping the unfortunate Mary a virtual prisoner, moving her around their many properties.

At Chatsworth, her lodgings, which are still referred to as the Queen of Scots apartments, were on the east side of the house and the rooms survived unaltered until their remodelling in the late 17th century. Then, most of the Elizabethan furniture, tapestries and paintings that Mary would have been familiar with, were taken to Hardwick Hall, a complete Elizabethan setting ready to receive them.

Some people feel that Mary would have left a strong imprint in these apartments, but we have no record of her psychic energy here. A spirit presence has been felt, but it is an older lady with an autocratic manner, believed to be the ghost of Evelyn, the wife of the 9th Duke of Devonshire. A beautiful needlewoman, for 50 years the Duchess carefully restored many rare embroideries and tapestries, and now her ghost is said to be still taking the responsibility of caring for Chatsworth very seriously.

Apparently the present Dowager Duchess has experienced several phantoms within the building. Doors have been seen to open and close by themselves, footsteps, muffled voices, banging, clattering and thumping noises have been heard. Ghostly ladies have been seen wandering along the corridors and through various rooms, and in the library, the Duchess is said to have watched an opaque phantom glide about the room.

Bess of Hardwick's ghost is believed to haunt the building and the grounds, but the most often-reported sighting is of Mary, Queen of Scots around what is

Queen Mary's Bower.

now known as Queen Mary's Bower. When she was imprisoned at Chatsworth, this was one of her favourite haunts. It would appear that it still is, as her unhappy spirit has been seen ascending the steps and walking around the area immediately in front.

BEELEY

On the edge of Gibbet Moor is Hob Hurst's House, one of the least-known pre-historic sites in Derbyshire. Its unusual name is derived from Hob – an elf or goblin, and Hurst – the old word for a wood, so by combining the two we have the dwelling of a hobgoblin in a wood. Hob was well known to our ancestors who would leave small quantities of food and drink in a special place to placate this spirit of nature. They believed that when Hob was good he was magical, but when upset, he could cause havoc and even eat children. When a pile of scorched human bones was discovered at Hob Hurst's House in an archaeological dig carried out by Thomas Bateman in June 1853, the legend took on a macabre element, and the place now has a reputation for being the haunt of demonic forces.

DARLEY MOOR

The Woodlands is an isolated property on Darley Moor with a history of mysterious fires which legend tells us can be traced back centuries, to when the site was occupied by a lonely wayside inn named The Quiet Woman. But the landlady was not just quiet, she was surly and sullen and her unpleasant attitude discouraged customers who stopped for sustenance and shelter. Some tales tell that not only did she discourage them, she made a habit of robbing and murdering them, then buried their bodies in the cellar.

Understandably, business became so bad that the landlord had to find some other form of employment, and turned to highway robbery to supplement his income. Then one dark night, this robber/landlord was wounded by his intended victim, who broke free and headed for the supposed safety of the inn.

A few minutes later, his injured assailant arrived home and was pushed into the cellar to hide. In the scuffle that ensued, an oil lamp was knocked over and fire spread rapidly across the room, trapping the unfortunate man in the cellar. The landlady escaped the fire but the experience left her deranged. Another version said she was hanged for her crimes, but returned to re-enact the accident for eternity.

The vastly altered building became a farmhouse, then in 1966 a country club known as Moor Lane Sporting Club, which stood on the site was gutted by fire. The owner confided to friends that he had experienced odd happenings and was especially concerned that his dog took fright for no apparent reason. He probably had reason to worry because during subsequent re-building, a caravan he used was also gutted by fire.

The property that now occupies the site gives little hint of its gruesome past.

FARLEY

F our hundred years ago, a woman and her children froze to death in a blizzard on the bleak Beeley Moors round Farley and Darley Hillside despite a desperate search by the distraught husband and father Henry Columbell. It is said that his ghost can still be heard on the first night of the full moon in March, as he continues his search, galloping round the area calling his wife's name.

HARTINGDON

O n 3rd December 1745, HRH Prince Charles Edward Stuart, better known as Bonnie Prince Charlie, accompanied by a bodyguard of Scottish lords, the music of bagpipes and an army of 7,000, was

Bonnie Prince Charlie.

leading the Jacobite Rebellion on their march to London, in an attempt to re-establish the Stuart succession.

Crossing the county border from Staffordshire to Derbyshire, the army would have used the River Dove as a navigational aid, and Hartington's position at the crossing of the Dove gave it strategic importance.

It is therefore not unreasonable to assume that the Prince was invited to share the hospitality of Hartington Hall, but he enjoyed more than just the usual generosity of the house. A certain bonny young maid caught his eye and being a loyal supporter, his wish was her command. The Prince stayed the night in what is now known as the Bonnie Prince Charlie Room, and next day as he rode away he promised to return for the maid once the political upheavals had died down.

He moved on to Derby and attended a special service at All Saint's church, now Derby Cathedral, where a plaque records the event, and his ghost is said to haunt the building. Ladies were eager to catch a glimpse of His Royal Highness who, at 24, was described as six feet tall with a majestic presence, but the undisciplined band of soldiers evoked both fear and pity. In advance of the main army, a group of 70 Scottish soldiers were sent to Swarkstone, seven miles south of Derby to secure the only bridge crossing the River Trent.

Charles stayed at Exeter House in Full Street, now the site of the police station, courtesy of the Earl of Exeter on the nights of 4th and 5th December. It was there in the drawing room that heated discussions took place. Charles

Derby Museum's Bonnie Prince Charlie Room.

wanted to continue the march south but his officers wanted to retreat. Eventually, in desperation, Charles had to accept defeat, as the decision was made to abandon their attempt to re-establish the Stuart succession, and Charles's dream of taking the English crown from George II.

On 6th December the advance guard at Swarkstone bridge were recalled and began their long march back to Scotland. But have they left a lasting legacy? Many people report hearing the sound of horse's hooves and the accompanying clatter of armour and swords around Swarkstone Bridge, although the ghostly cavalry never materialise.

Sadly, Bonnie Prince Charlie never did return and the maid died of a broken heart, but even then she kept up her vigil. Visitors to Hartington Hall, one of the first youth hostels in the country, opened in 1934, have reported seeing her ghost wandering from room to room peering at the sleeping occupants, apparently looking for her prince.

Exeter House was destroyed in 1854, but the drawing room's panelling was saved and reinstated in Derby Museum in what is now known as the Bonnie Prince Charlie Room. People have reported feeling a sense of depression and foreboding in this room, as if the panelling has retained the despair that Charles Edward Stewart experienced that night.

YOULGREAVE

The skirmishes that took place between the Cavaliers and Roundheads during the Civil War have certainly left their mark, not only on our history but on our psychic landscape. Ghosts in the distinctive uniform of each side turn up quite regularly, but Youlgreave Hall can expand upon that. Their Civil War visitors are a Cavalier and a Roundhead who reputedly fought to the death one dark November night back in the 1640s in one of the Hall's bedrooms.

Since then, the ghostly clashing of swords has been heard on a regular basis, re-enacted on each anniversary in what is now referred to as the Duel Room.

*   *   *

If you take the road from Middleton to Youlgreave, watch out for a phantom coach and horses lit by eerie lamps and accompanied by ghostly dogs. One witness is said to have felt the wind as it passed, but assuming you make it to the neighbouring village of Birchover, head for the Druid Inn.

This is a name to conjure up all sorts of visions, and in the past, Druid worship is believed to have taken place in the nearby Rowter Rocks, now haunted by many malevolent spirits. A cloaked, ghostly figure is the most frequently seen, although on moonlit nights it is said that the whole area is filled with the sound of weeping and wailing. It is therefore rather reassuring that the Druid Inn is reputedly haunted by a kindly old lady. She is said to have a warm, caring smile and sits in the corner of one of the downstairs rooms.

*   *   *

Just a short walk from here is the notorious Stanton Moor where witches still meet. This area is rich in stone circles, burial mounds and other remnants of an ancient era, including a votive tree which is still used today. Tie a strip of your clothing to the tree, repeat your wish three times and I'm assured it will be granted.

There are many stories of strange experiences on the moor. These include abduction by UFOs, reports of a spectral black dog with flaming eyes, huge teeth and a foaming mouth, a ghostly monk, a headless horseman, a green man, a white lady and hovering lights called 'will o' the wisp' or corpse candles, said by some to foretell death.

Even modern day witches report a strong feeling of evil in the area, particularly round the Nine Ladies Circle. The circle is 35ft in diameter and to

The yew tree in the churchyard at Darley Dale is estimated to be 2,000 years old.

the south west is the King's stone, also known as The Fiddler's Chair. According to legend, the devil played his fiddle while nine ladies danced on the Sabbath. God was so furious that he turned them into stone for disregarding his holy day. A ghostly male figure dressed in black has often been seen standing just outside the circle. Could this be the devil, or the fiddler, or just a trick of the light?

Leaving Stanton Moor and crossing the River Derwent at Darley Bridge, the first turning on your left is known as Ghost Lane. It was here that in the 17th century, a Scottish peddler was robbed and murdered. Ever since, his ghost is said to haunt the area between the large sycamore tree and the churchyard where you will find the largest yew tree in England, estimated to be 2,000 years old.

WINSTER

The main street of the old mining town of Winster is lined with attractive stone buildings, and amongst them is Winster Hall, an impressive Georgian house, which is associated with a rather tragic lover's leap.

Supposedly, many years ago, the daughter of the house fell in love with a coachman, but her parents objected to the match. They arranged for her to marry someone they considered more suitable for a lady in her position but, on the eve of the wedding, the lovers climbed to the top of the house and clinging to each other, jumped from the parapet to their deaths.

The young lovers were buried opposite the door of Winster church but the wraith of this unhappy girl is still said to haunt the forecourt of the hall.

Further down the road is the old Market Hall, the first building in the county to be owned by the National Trust, and opposite is a three-storey house formerly called the Angel Inn although its name belied its reputation. A murder supposedly took place in one of the bedrooms, probably a strangulation, as some time ago, a lady sleeping in that room woke convinced that she was being choked by ghostly hands.

There are accounts of doors opening and closing and ghostly footsteps, but the most bizarre story is that of the headless bride. One day a lady was sitting at her dressing table. The door to the landing was open and through the mirror, she saw a white clad figure descending the stairs. The figure was dressed as a bride but as she moved further down the stairs, it was obvious that she had no head. As she turned and walked into the room, the lady at her dressing table fainted.

The question is asked 'Why are so many ghosts headless?'

The most obvious

Winster Hall.

explanation would be that they were beheaded, accidentally or otherwise, and the sudden shock traumatised the spirit to such an extent that it is imprinted on the fabric of time. Alternatively, archaeological excavations of Pagan, Celtic and Saxon burial grounds, have revealed that some of the human remains had their heads removed and placed between their knees or feet. This was common practise in the belief that this would stop their spirits rising from the grave. From the number of headless ghosts we encounter, it obviously didn't work too well!

• North-east Derbyshire •

DRONFIELD

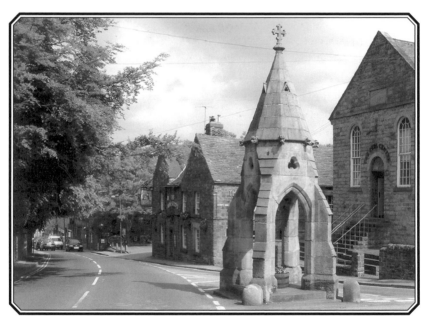

The Peel Monument, with the Blue Stoops pub, the haunt of a young girl, beyond.

Dronfield is in the eastern foothills of the Pennines and is the largest township in north-east Derbyshire. It is completely surrounded by green-belt, yet it is only a few miles from the sprawling suburbs of

Sheffield. Residential development has been consolidated mainly in the neighbouring communities of Dronfield Woodhouse and Coal Aston, allowing Dronfield to retain its ancient character and its many fine old buildings. Standing in the heart of the old centre and at the site of the former cross and stocks, is the impressive Peel Monument, a tribute to Sir Robert Peel's attempts to abolish the Corn Laws in 1846.

Behind the Peel monument is the Manor House, now the Dronfield library, reputed to have a white lady who haunts the upper floor. She is believed to be a servant girl who died in 1711. A short distance away is the Hall, built in the reign of Queen Anne. Now a private residence, it has a fair number of ghosts and considerable poltergeist activity, plus reports of the ghost of a white lady seen in the adjoining gardens. Could it be a different white lady or the same one who has strolled down from the library?

Although there is little evidence now of Dronfield's medieval past, the Green Dragon pub and the Chantry Hotel were part of Beauchief Abbey. It wasn't until after the dissolution of the monasteries and the subsequent suppression of the guilds and chantries in 1547, that they became separate establishments. A stone archway was discovered during recent renovation work, linking the two, but what they also have in common is a ghost with a penchant for turning the gas cylinder taps off. The Chantry Hotel also has poltergeist activity where glasses are hurled through the air and plates smashed.

Another ancient inn, not far away, is the Blue Stoops, built in the 1590s. It is said that a young girl was murdered there and now haunts the building.

Although the actual building dates back to the 16th century, the Manor Hotel on the High Street was only made into a hotel in the late 1960s. It was originally four separate cottages and it is in the part that was once number ten where most of the ghostly activity takes place. It is believed to be the haunt of an old lady who lived there at the turn of the 19th century. Both visitors and staff have sensed her presence and many have actually seen her and been able to describe her as about 70 years old, wearing long skirts, laced boots and tied back hair. Occasionally they feel her touching them or clinging to their arms. Sometimes she rattles the pots and pans or moves the ornaments on the shelves but generally she is described as being a friendly spirit, and no trouble at all.

Several years ago, a human skeleton was given to the Dronfield branch of St John Ambulance. It was intended to be used for demonstration purposes, yet is there a link between its presence and the unexplained phenomena that has been happening at the St John Ambulance office in Dronfield? Lights in the building flicker and doors are said to slam shut without explanation. One long-term member of the group can relate many incidents of heavy footsteps when there was no one around, and once he heard the downstairs door open and someone enter the building. He called a greeting, but when there was no reply, he went to investigate and found that he was alone.

The strangest incident happened in the late 1970s when a presentation was held on the premises. Two members with Polaroid cameras decided to record the event with a group photograph, but both photographs came out blank. Later, a further photograph was taken, but as it began to develop it was soon obvious that this was the photograph taken earlier. No-one can explain what happened, but as they looked at the photograph, they were even more mystified because there was an extra person present, a bearded phantom.

Where he came from was a mystery. The local and national newspapers soon got hold of the story. The Superintendent and his wife were interviewed, the photograph examined and eventually the bearded gentleman was identified as the victim of a road accident 150 years earlier.

ECKINGTON

Home of the Sitwell family for over 350 years, Renishaw Hall is set in parkland on the south-eastern outskirts of Eckington. In recent decades the house has become famous through the writings of Edith, Osbert and Sacheverell, the three gifted children of Sir George and Lady Ida Sitwell.

It is now the family home of Sir Reresby Sitwell, seventh baronet of Renishaw and Lady Sitwell, but in the beginning of the 18th century, it was home to Henry, the last of the Sacheverells, a sickly child who died in 1726, aged thirteen. Sadly, Henry seemed loathe to leave his family home and remained in spirit. He was known as 'The Little Boy in Pink', who had a penchant for nestling up to lady guests and giving them three cold kisses. Apparently various ladies sleeping alone in a certain bedroom were disturbed by this light touch.

In the 1890s Sir George Sitwell decided to re-build the staircase and make it larger by knocking down one wall of the previously mentioned bedroom to incorporate it and the room below into the staircase. It was then that they found a lid-less coffin fastened by iron clamps to the joists under the bedroom floorboards. There were no bones in the coffin but it had definite marks that suggested it had once contained a body.

Henry Sacheverell is believed to haunt a certain bedroom.

Twenty years later, Lady Ida Sitwell, Sir George's wife, was resting on a sofa in the upstairs drawing room talking to friends after dinner. Facing the open door, she saw a grey-haired woman wearing a white cap and a crinoline dress, walk along the corridor with a slow, gliding motion. The figure headed straight towards the head of the old staircase and vanished at the spot where the door to the haunted room had once been.

BARLBOROUGH HALL

B arlborough Hall is a Grade I listed building built in 1583 for Francis Rodes by Robert Smythson who also worked as the architect of Hardwick Hall. There is a similarity in style, but Barlborough Hall has the rare distinction of being a compact, almost square Elizabethan mansion. Now a school, the Hall has retained many original features like the Great Chamber which is now the chapel with its impressive double fireplace flanked by figures of Wisdom and Justice. This is a fitting tribute both to its original owner Sir Frances Rodes, a judge in the Court of Common Pleas, and said to be one of the judges who tried Mary Queen of Scots, and to the principles of the Jesuit school that now occupies the building. This Roman Catholic religious order arrived secretly in England in 1580 to set up a school for the education of boys who would otherwise not receive a Catholic education. Many of its students went on to become priests and sometimes gave their lives for their faith.

Barlborough Hall.

In 1939, Barlborough Hall with its 320-acre estate, became the preparatory school to Mount St Mary's College, Spinkhill, founded in 1842, but at the centre of Jesuit activity from the very earliest times.

Like that of the Jesuits, the hall's history is also tangled with religious persecution. Above and at the side of the main entrance can be seen the spy holes of the priest hide, used during the 16th century to conceal Catholic priests. Sadly this wasn't always successful and the ghost of a recusant priest, murdered while in concealment, is said to haunt an upper room. Despite many attempts to remove them, his bloodstains are alleged to have left indelible stains on the floor of the room.

CHESTERFIELD

There are many stories categorised as urban legends that have replaced and updated our traditional folklore. This is one of them. It was a wild, wintry night and the last bus to Chesterfield had left its official stop in Whitwell and was going along the road towards the church. The wipers were busy keeping the sleet and snow from the windscreen and the driver had almost passed when he saw a man standing outside one of the cottages with his arm outstretched to halt the bus. Although this was not a regulation stop, in country districts, the drivers use their discretion and, bearing in mind the dreadful weather, this driver pulled over to admit the man who ascended the stairs to the upper deck.

The only thing the driver thought unusual at the time was the man's dry clothes considering the wet weather, but a few minutes later when the conductress ascended the stairs to collect his fare, the passenger had vanished. The other passengers said he had gone to the back of the bus, but a search failed to reveal his whereabouts. The driver was understandably distressed by this, but the conductress was so distraught, she suffered a nervous illness and never returned to work. Was this a mental mirage? If evidence of a psychic phenomena is based on only one person's account, there might be grounds for sceptical suspicion, but when two or more people witness the same manifestation and their testimonies agree in every detail, it can't be dismissed quite so easily.

Tapton House was the much-loved home of George Stephenson, the 'Railway King' who leased it in 1838 until his death on 12th August 1848. Such was the respect in which he was held, both nationally and locally, that on the day of his funeral, all the shops of Chesterfield were closed. He was laid to rest at Holy Trinity Church but probably 'laid to rest' are inappropriate words considering the number of times he has been seen since, and the most sightings have been at Tapton House.

In the 1920s the young daughter of a footman employed at Tapton House played regularly in the grounds but, on one occasion, she and her friend ventured into the old coachhouse and climbed into a neglected coach to play. After a while, they became aware of an old gentleman standing in the corner

Tapton House.

watching them. He was of medium height, but appeared taller because of the tall, 'stove-pipe' hat he was wearing. The girls left in a hurry and fearing a reprimand were reluctant to tell their parents. When they did eventually confess, the footman professed that he too had seen the ghost on many occasions. It was the great man himself, George Stephenson.

From 1931 to 1993 Tapton House was a school, and apparently there were many sightings during this time. On one occasion, a caretaker was sweeping a corridor on the first floor when she heard a masculine voice say quite clearly, 'You didn't bring my water up today!'

She looked up to see a total stranger. He was dressed in old-fashioned clothing, but he was quite normal in every other aspect. When he repeated the words, she made a

George Stephenson haunts his former home.

mumbled apology and hurried off to find her husband. After telling him what had just happened, they returned to the now empty corridor. The only way the man could have left was through a locked door at the end of the corridor, but the door was still locked. Later when shown a selection of photographs taken from portraits, without hesitation, the caretaker selected the portrait of George Stephenson as the man she had seen.

After a considerable revamp, in 1994 Tapton House was taken over by the Chesterfield College of Further and Higher Education who are still there today, but the sightings did not stop. Over the last few years, there have been reports of doors mysteriously opening and closing, and masculine footsteps on the corridors. One former student told me that a portrait of George Stephenson that hangs in the hall has eyes that follow you around. Is this a vivid imagination or is George still keeping an eye on his old home?

*   *   *

A bell-ringer in the ringing room of the parish church of St Mary and All Saints, Chesterfield, better known as the Crooked Spire, was suddenly aware of a quiet shuffling sound in the bell-chamber directly above him, then one of the ten bell ropes began to swing erratically. Without stopping for a second, he shot downstairs and alerted the verger who rang the police. Three constables and a sergeant arrived and despite a thorough check of the bell chamber, found nothing. Mystified, the group then checked the ringing room where they discovered a dead sparrow at the foot of one of the ropes. In its dying moments the bird must have fluttered across the floor, clung to one of the ropes, then fallen through to the room below.

The Crooked Spire, Chesterfield.

If only everything could be explained so neatly! On several occasions people in the ringing room have heard footsteps approaching quickly from the stairwell. On each occasion no one appeared and despite making a systematic search, there was never anyone there.

A couple of senior choristers saw a small, white shape hovering in the vestry and although it was featureless, they felt instinctively that it was a figure dressed in a shroud. It drifted from the outside wall of the vestry towards a closed door that opened into the church where it simply melted.

Talbot Dilworth-Harrison, Priest Vicar of the parish and Archdeacon of Chesterfield 1934–63, died on 16th May 1975 aged 88. His ashes are interred in the vault below the Italian marble floor tablet in his memory, but his spirit has been sensed and his ghost seen by lady stewards in the area of the Holy Cross Chapel.

*   *   *

During the early years of the 19th century when the Old Manor House in New Square was still a private residence, a lady saw a small child in the corridor. Thinking that the infant must have somehow wandered in off the street, she reached out to take the tiny hand and was horrified when her arm passed through the ethereal body.

Another previous occupant heard a ghost with clanking chains walk across the hall and into the dining room. Thinking to imprison the fettered phantom in there, she quickly locked the door, but this proved to be no deterrent; the intruder clanked noisily out again.

Now the building is the Chesterfield premises of Yorkshire Bank, where unexplained incidents seemed to centralise around the manager's office on the ground floor. An ex-manager is reported to have experienced strange happenings in what was undoubtedly the previous dining room on the right of the front door. One member of the bank staff told me that whenever she went into this room, the pictures were always hanging on a slant despite the number of times she straightened them. Was this a playful ghost?

The building was completely refurbished and officially reopened on 17th May 1999 by Michael Fanshawe, Mayor of Chesterfield to celebrate Yorkshire Bank's one hundred years in Chesterfield. With the alterations, the room previously used by the manager was allocated to be used to house the mechanics of the mini bank, but did this stop the activity? Not according to the lady who services the mini bank. She has experienced some very bizarre incidents when filling it up.

BOLSOVER CASTLE

This fairy-tale castle perched on a ridge commands the most magnificent views over the valley of the M1 motorway. Its long history goes back to the days of William the Conqueror who gave the site to his illegitimate son William Peverel. During the 15th and 16th centuries, the castle passed back and forth between noble and royal hands until in 1553 it was granted to George Talbot, later Earl of Shrewsbury and the fourth husband of Bess of Hardwick. In 1608, Bess's favourite son Sir Charles Cavendish leased it from his stepbrother and began building the 'Keep' or 'Little Castle'. Sir Charles died in 1617 so the completion, including the fashionable decoration, was added by his son Sir William Cavendish.

Sir William Cavendish belonged to an elite group of horsemen skilled in ceremonial tournaments and had a pre-occupation with all things equestrian. He built the riding house to enable him to show off his skills and his ghost may still be there doing just that. The sound of horses has been heard by security guards, lights move around as if someone is carrying a candle and footsteps have been heard on the top floor when no one has been there. The dummy boards of William Cavendish and his lady have been known to move on their own, and the electrical equipment, recordings and lights switch themselves on and off.

Walking around the castle, many visitors experience a feeling of being watched or pushed along by an invisible force. Some see Civil War soldiers marching up and down the Terrace Range, others have heard the sound of marching feet and trotting horses coming up the south drive.

Ghostly knights have been seen walking around the thick wall that surrounds the fountain garden, and the apparition of a grey lady walks through an archway in the wall, an archway that was built up in 1630. But the most appealing spectre of all is the little boy. He has been seen joining visiting children in the fountain garden. He is known to take their hands although the families are normally quite oblivious to him.

In the Little Castle, Sir William's favourite room was the Elysium Room where people have experienced the scent of pipe-smoke and perfume. One

The dummy boards in the riding house are frequently moved by ghostly hands. Note the circles of light caught on the right of this photograph, could they be light anomalies?

member of staff finishing a guided tour was joking about Sir William being a bit of a ladies' man, when something physically pushed her down the stairs causing her to hurt her ankle. All around the castle there have been incidents involving people being slapped, tickled, pinched or their clothes being tugged in a childish or familiar fashion.

By far the most active room is the wooden floored room that was last occupied by Mrs Robbins, the housekeeper to the Revd Hamilton Grey who lived at the castle in the late 19th century. Problems have been encountered when trying to enter and exit this room as it seems that the ghostly housekeeper is in the habit of locking the door to keep people out. Here staff and visitors have experienced doors closing, strange opaque mists, a feeling of tightness in the chest and breathing difficulties. Mrs Robbins died of some form of pneumonia and there is sometimes a dusty quality in the air in that room.

Visitors report feeling claustrophobic and a figure believed to be Mrs Robbins has been seen in the corner of the room.

From the top floor, 100 service stairs descend directly to the pre-1617 vaulted basement with many original kitchen features. Apparently one visitor some time ago remarked to the then custodian Peggy White, that she had just passed Sir Charles Cavendish on the stairs. 'Well he shouldn't be here,' Peggy replied firmly, 'these are the servants' quarters.'

The smell of oranges is often strong in the kitchen, and some people have reported smelling cucumber and other foodstuffs. There are also strange noises and lots of slaps and pinches administered in this area. It is thought that there was once a dungeon under the beer cellar. Stamp and it sounds very hollow!

A medium, who stayed one night at Bolsover Castle, later reported having seen many unruly happenings including the most frightening of all apparitions at Bolsover Castle. Apparently, a young woman hurried through the kitchen carrying a bundle in her arms. As she entered the side room dominated by the ovens, she glanced around, opened an oven door and thrust the bundle inside. As she did so, a baby screamed and as the screams faded away, so did the ghostly woman. The medium had witnessed a baby being burnt to death in the kitchen ovens.

STAVELEY

It has been said that any place where people have lived is likely to house a ghost. Whether the inhabitants are aware of it or not is another matter, although certain individuals will sense rather than see. Light anomalies, also known as orbs, are the first stages of a ghost manifestation. These have been caught on film, but people are more likely to see a mist or shadows. These formless, spiritual entities have not learnt how to build up the energy to give a discernible face or features, but once they have they come in every shape and form.

The most regularly seen are white ladies, either because they are wearing a shroud or because they seem to exude a radiance or glow from their ghostly, diaphanous bodies. One such lady is Frances Culpepper who for many years haunted The Hagge, near Staveley. Her poignant story touched the heart of an unknown local poet who wrote this rather lovely verse, immortalising her forever. It is included here in homage to all the ghostly white ladies of Derbyshire.

As you cross the entrance hall to ascend the oaken stair
Fear not to meet the lady who hath oft-times lingered there.

In cloak and hat of antique guise and robes of purest white
She vanished from the gazer's sight, e'en in the noontime light.

Surely she was a blessed sprite who then did churchward go
No traces left of passing steps upon the stainless snow.

A serving man obeisance made as to one of mortal mould
With look unchanged she passed him by, her eyes were fixed and cold.

None stayed her step, none questioned her, for her lips were mute and pale
And a snow-white greyhound followed, fleet as the passing gale.

They glimmered through the midnight gloom ere the last of name and race
Was borne away from her lonely couch to the grave's cold resting place.

ASHOVER

'Ghoulish goings-on at a North Derbyshire pub are really putting customers in the Halloween spirit' reports the Derbyshire Times – 26th October 1995.

The article is about the 15th century Crispin Inn at Ashover that is rumoured to be haunted by no fewer than seventeen ghosts, including monks, cavaliers, itinerants, animals, former landlords and children.

Ashover from the churchyard with the Crispin in the foreground.

Early records of the Crispin, show that it was the residence of the Wall family, publicans and shoe-makers, hence the inn's name. St Crispin is the patron saint of cobblers, saddlers and harness makers, the main occupation of most of the men of the village centuries ago.

One member of the family is immortalised on the large plaque outside the inn stating that in 1646, during the Civil War, Job Wall refused admittance to the King's men, as they had had too much drink already. They ignored him, threw him out and posted a guard on the door while they drank the ale-house dry.

Jumping 3½ centuries, in July 2004 the Crispin was taken over by new owners who almost immediately set about architectural surgery. Retaining its authentic ambience, they have not only achieved a transformation that is sympathetic to the building, they have also disturbed the ghosts.

Workmen have been traumatised by numerous unnerving experiences and admitted that they regularly felt something or someone behind them giving them a push.

With the completion of the work, customers have reported feeling a drop in temperature or a cool draught, often referred to as a psychic breeze. This is surprisingly common. It is believed that heat is converted into metaphysical energy that causes manifestation or supernatural activity to take place.

On one occasion, the background music suddenly blurted out at full volume. No one had been near the music centre, yet the knob had been turned to maximum.

The licensees, Robert and Andrew, have had their own experiences. Andrew, who has two young children, was convinced a child had thrown its arms round his legs, but when he reached down and turned around, he was alone.

*　　*　　*

Further along Church Street in Ashover is the Black Swan, where two previous licensees and family members have seen the ghostly figure of a woman walk along an upper corridor and simply melt into the end wall. A Cavalier is also said to haunt the Black Swan but the present landlady suggests it might have simply left the Crispin because it's a bit crowded down there.

*　　*　　*

An empty stone coffin dating from around 1200 was unearthed in Ashover churchyard many years ago, and supposedly, if you walk round this three times, then lie in it with your eyes closed, you will hear the ghostly sounds of rattling chains. I went to check this out for myself, on a bright sunny day, (coward that I am), but my plans were thwarted. I found the empty stone sarcophagus lying at the base of the church tower, but as it was too close to the wall of the church, there was no way anyone could walk round it.

The churchyard is also the haunt of a headless woman, believed to be the ghost of the wife of John Townrow, a 60-year-old farmer from Milltown who on 10th June 1841 bludgeoned her to death, cut off her head, then slit his own throat.

The empty coffin in Ashover churchyard.

This headless ghost is often linked with the story of the Stubben Edge skull, although there is no connection other than the obvious. Supposedly at a supper party held at Stubben Edge Hall in 1850, a wager was made that no one would dare go to Ashover graveyard and bring back a skull. Macabre though this now sounds, it was once the fashion to collect and display unusual and grotesque artefacts, the more macabre the piece of ornamentation the better, and skulls were much in demand. The story of Dicky O' Tunstead, a skull that acted as cranial guardian of a farm overlooking Coombs reservoir up in the High Peak for 350 years, gained national acclaim for its supposed antics.

At the time, there was also a widely practised belief in the science of phrenology, the study of the shape and size of the skull to determine the strength of various mental faculties. Whatever the reason for making the wager, one of the young Milnes boys who resided at the Hall, took up the challenge and returned with the skull from Ashover churchyard.

Thirty years later (1889), while building a conservatory at Stubben Edge Hall, the skull was found and returned to the churchyard. It would seem that the ghost of Mrs Townrow could at last rest in peace as the last official sighting of her, witnessed by a local, was in 1890 in the north aisle of the church at 8 pm.

*　　*　　*

Eastwood Hall on the outskirts of Ashover village, was a casualty of the Civil War and is now a crumbling ruin. As Leonard Wheatcroft, poet and Clerk to the Church wrote at the time –

> The Roundheads came down upon Eastwood Old Hall
> And they tried it with mattock and tried it with ball
> And they tore up the leadwork and splintered the wood
> But as firmly as ever, the battlements stood
> Till a barrel of powder at last did the thing
> And then they sang psalms for the fall of the King.

In recent years, the ghost of a Cavalier has been seen near these ruins and six horseshoes were found in the snow in 2000. The style of the shoe, with a central band, was used during the Civil War on horses that pulled heavy artillery like cannon.

*   *   *

Many years ago, a man set out along the Uppertown/Kelstedge Road in search of a doctor for his wife who was about to give birth. It was a dreadfully foggy night and unable to find a doctor, he returned to find his wife and baby had died. He was said to be devastated and died within the year, but does he still haunt the lane?

In 1948, Dr Simon Bell was called out one night at 1.30 am and travelling along this lane, he suddenly encountered a fog so dense it was impossible to continue his journey. He could see nothing outside, but then it started to creep into his car and choke him. Dr Bell was a logical man and he knew this was not natural. Just as he was about to panic, the mist cleared and he drove away as fast as he could.

Had Dr Bell experienced some sort of replay of the former emotive event, triggered by the fog and the fact that he was a doctor? Did a combination of the conditions on that earlier night find a way to record themselves at this particular location, then replay to produce a quite curious phenomena? We can never be sure, but experts all agree that a mist like this is the first manifestation of a ghost.

*   *   *

Goss Hall, or Gorse Hall as it was formerly known, dates back to the 16th century and stands above the village of Ashover on the coach road to Overton Hall. It was originally owned by the Deincourt family and eventually passed to a member of the Babington family. Anthony Babington is said to have taken refuge in the cellar of Goss Hall following the discovery of his plot to rescue Mary, Queen of Scots from Wingfield Manor.

The Hall is also said to have belonged to Sir Walter Raleigh for a short time prior to this, so is it surprising that it should have a ghost that smokes a pipe which fills the house with tobacco smoke? (Sir Walter introduced tobacco to this country.)

Goss Hall may have the pipe-smoking ghost of Sir Walter Raleigh.

The smell was apparently so bad in the 1950s that it caused one owner to leave, and although it became almost a ruin, Goss Hall is now a very desirable private house.

Phantom fragrance, or abstract odours as they are frequently called, are often associated with spirit activity, and it is not uncommon to detect abstract odours when dealing with the paranormal. These can be pleasant or pungent, and people have smelt all manner of things.

Like all other mysterious psychic phenomena, how it happens is a complete mystery to which we can apply no logical explanation. All we know is that the departed are somehow able to activate our sense of smell as a means of communicating with us.

Overton Hall and its grounds of approximately 1,000 acres originally belonged to the Overton family. The estate was handed to the Hunts in 1327, then in 1599 purchased by William Hodgkinson of Northedge. This thirty-roomed

Overton Hall.

mansion passed by marriage to the Banks family and so to Sir Joseph Banks, the distinguished naturalist.

At the age of eighteen, Joseph Banks came into a considerable inheritance enabling him to pursue his keen interest in botany in adventurous style. In 1766 he undertook the first of his discovery voyages to Newfoundland, was made a Fellow of the Royal Society, then from 1768–71 accompanied Captain James Cook aboard HMS Endeavour acting as the supervisory scientist on the Royal Society's famed expedition to the South Seas. They returned with a vast collection of botanical specimens, and Sir Joseph planted a wide variety of rare trees and shrubs in the parklands and grounds of Overton Hall.

But things more sinister than plants were buried there. In 1884 when digging the foundations for a wall, 27 skeletons were unearthed. All were big, heavy men with their skulls broken. They were re-interred in Ashover churchyard but nothing was discovered to throw any light on the reason for the rather unorthodox burial in the grounds at Overton. Some reports say they appeared to have been buried hastily, perhaps as a result of plague but that would not account for their damaged skulls.

Sir Joseph died on 19th June 1820 without issue and the property passed to John Bright Esq then the Jessop family. After that, this once fine residence was used as a youth hostel in the 1930s, a boarding school for boys evacuated from Derby during the first part of the War, then an approved school, followed by a residential home for the elderly.

In 1956, a story was reported in the press that the wife of a Pentecostal pastor living at Overton Hall had left because it was haunted. The figure of a woman, thought to be the third wife of one of the Jessops is said to haunt the forecourt. Perhaps she doesn't approve of the way the property has fared over the years, but as it is now converted into residential apartments, she may be able to rest in peace at last.

*   *   *

One evening a car containing four women was travelling between Ashover and Woolley Moor. It was about 8 pm on a March evening, so the night was

54

dark and visibility poor on the unlit country road but, at the crossroads on the stretch overlooking Ogston reservoir, they encountered a small, headless figure, dressed in an off-white smock. According to the report, there was only the outline of a head and the figure was waving its arms around disjointedly.

The car's occupants panicked and drove off, although they later returned but saw nothing. There have been other sightings of this ghost at the same crossroads, but who she was or why she was there remains a mystery.

Crossroads seem to be a favourite haunt of ghosts. One theory is that witches were believed to hold orgies and practise the black art at crossroads and, in doing so, may have conjured up some strange apparitions.

An alternative idea is that murderers, suspect witches and suicides were buried at crossroads to emphasise their marginal status in society. Then, there is the Christian belief that crossroads were used because the cross was a form of protection from demons, vampires and supernatural night creatures, and just to be on the safe side, many were buried with a stake thrust through them in an attempt to keep their spirits from wandering.

TUPTON

One Sunday morning in 1981, a young woman from Tupton was taking her dog for a walk when she came across an old cottage she hadn't noticed before. She had a sudden urge to explore the ruin which was overgrown with vegetation and falling down. As it had no doors or windows, she was able to walk inside and examine each derelict room. Her dog joined her, sniffing the unfamiliar structure and showing no signs of agitation or fear.

Returning home, the woman told her husband about the old cottage, but he insisted there was no such place. To settle the argument, they set off in their car, but when they reached the spot, the woman could only stand and stare in disbelief. The cottage was no longer there. Prompted by curiosity, they obtained some old maps of the area and on one was the old cottage.

SUTTON SCARSDALE

Lying close to junction 29 of the M1 motorway at Heath, from a distance, Sutton Scarsdale Hall gives the impression of romantic splendour and was once said to be one of the finest houses of Derbyshire. It was an outstanding example of classical architecture built in 1724, designed by Francis Smith and commissioned by Nicholas Leake, 4th and last Earl of Sutton Scarsdale. Its interior was ornate and lavish, as were the gardens that surrounded the estate, yet now the great mansion is a crumbling ruin, a sad, melancholy shell, every bit the traditional haunted building.

The fine work of Italian craftsmen ravaged by time.

At one time owned by the Arkwright family, the hall was put up for sale in 1920, but no one wanted to live in this fabulous mansion. A speculator bought the property and desecrated it, selling lead from the roof and ripping out much of the interior. Ceilings began to collapse and the fine work of Italian craftsmen was ravaged by the weather, but fate intervened when Sir Osbert Sitwell agreed to purchase the building simply to save it from total destruction.

Now owned by English Heritage, the site has been cleaned and the building preserved, but it still retains its air of ghostly quiet disturbed only by the squawking black crows that circle the building and perch on the high walls to peer down. I found these rather disconcerting, as crows are believed to carry the spirit of humans on to the next level of existence.

For years there have been numerous tales of hauntings in the Hall, the grounds, the annexed church of St Mary, and in the old incorrectly-named Priory nearby. Reports of a ghost with no legs and wearing a white hood with slits for eyes caused so much interest that an article appeared in the Star newspaper on 29th June 1967. The rector of St Mary's church suggested the ghost was probably one of the large white owls that glide between the bushes and trees, and circle the hall at night, yet despite this possible explanation, attention still focused strongly on the probability that Sutton Scarsdale Hall was haunted.

People report hearing phantom footsteps and voices, and feeling a distinctly eerie atmosphere. A grey-looking figure has been seen walking towards the back of the church and white lights and fleeting shadows flash across the windowless voids of this once great house.

HARDWICK HALL

Hardwick Hall will always be synonymous with its creator, that great Elizabethan lady, Bess of Hardwick. It is a wonderfully unspoilt relic of the past, partly due to the fact that since 1700, Chatsworth, not Hardwick has been the principal Derbyshire home of Bess's descendants, and thus has escaped alteration due to changing needs or fashion.

The indomitable Bess not only built this impressive mansion 400 years ago, she is still being seen wandering around it. In the stately rooms of the south wing, where Bess had her own private apartments, housekeeper Mrs Frances Stent was woken in her bedroom by the figure of Bess standing over her. 'She spoke kindly to me and thanked me for looking after her house and its contents so beautifully,' said Mrs Stent.

There have been reports of a presence being felt in the doorway by the chapel, and staff have frequently testified to seeing the figure of a lady dressed in blue wandering round the building, oblivious to the fact that people were watching her.

Phantom aromas have been noted in the 'High Chamber' where the

Bess of Hardwick,
Countess of Shrewsbury.

fragrance of citrus or other exotic fruits sometimes predominates.

A ghost cat is said to favour the Needlework Room and the Chapel landing but, according to one lady custodian, the Blue Bedroom is the centre of all the hauntings. Visitors to this room frequently report the feeling of being watched, while others claim to have been touched or spoken to by an invisible entity. Many people say there is a presence within the room, which is often icy cold, and the bed is frequently found to have an indentation as if some unseen individual has been lying there. One visitor reported seeing a young woman dressed in grey standing by the fireplace. The figure walked across the room, straight through the rope barrier that marked the public route and disappeared as she reached the bed.

A parachute regiment was billeted at Hardwick in 1942. One September evening, the sentry on the South Gate saw an unfamiliar figure walking towards him and called out 'Halt; who goes there?' The figure neither answered nor stopped, so the sentry raised the alarm before lunging forward with his bayonet, but the weapon met no resistance and the figure kept walking until it disappeared into Hardwick Hall. All the guards present at that incident described the figure as indistinct, but wearing a ruff collar and large plumed hat, the type of clothing worn by Royalist Cavaliers during the Civil War.

Some time later, a paratroop regiment approaching the triangle near Hardstoft saw a figure dressed in a ruff and a large plumed hat sitting on the wooden fence. Unable to believe their eyes, they slowed their pace as the figure slowly melted away. Sightings of the Cavalier have been a regular occurrence at Hardwick Hall but perhaps the most seen is a monk-like figure described as having a white, featureless face and wearing a black cowl.

*   *   *

There are rumoured to be several ghosts that haunt Hardwick Old Hall. One is the famous philosopher Thomas Hobbes of Malmesbury who lived and taught there, until he died at the age of 91. He is said to walk the drive and the perimeter of the old Hall, especially the path leading down to the present shop.

According to staff and visitors, there is one room in the West Lodge of Hardwick Old Hall that makes them feel uncomfortable. Dogs don't like it either. They have been known to go to the far corner of this room and bark at something only they can see or sense. West Lodge was used as a schoolroom at some point in the past, so staff now put any strange experiences down to mischievous, ghostly children playing tricks.

*   *   *

Josie, an experienced teacher, told me of her encounter with a ghost at a Victorian school on the eastern side of the county, an incident she can still vividly remember and can find no solution for.

She was teaching a class of children, when one child got up and walked out of the room. It was customary for a child wanting to leave the room to put their hand up first to obtain permission, yet this child had simply got up and walked out.

'The child who has just left the room,' Josie asked the classroom assistant, 'did they ask permission?'

'What child?' asked the other lady.

Josie looked at her in surprise, but it was obvious she had not seen the child. Josie however was adamant that she herself had. She did a head count and checked the register but all the children in the class were present.

So what had she seen? As she said, if the child was in any way different, she would have noticed immediately, but there was nothing abnormal about the child or the situation that might have raised suspicions, or the hair on the back of her neck.

•South-west Derbyshire•

CROMFORD

In 1769, a Lancashire barber and wig-maker had a bright idea for the mass production of yarn and cloth. He moved to Nottingham and built his first horse-powered mill, but soon he had the patent for a new invention, a water-powered cotton mill. What he needed was a reliable, constant and controllable source of water – which he found at Cromford where he could harness the energy and intensity of the River Derwent.

Having chosen his location, in 1771 Richard Arkwright set about building the first successful, water-powered cotton mill which was to start the transformation of textile manufacturing from a cottage industry to a factory-based industry. In 1776, a second, much larger mill was established on the site using the same water supply and soon there were water-powered mills dotted all along our main rivers.

The labour force was originally drawn from the local farming and mining communities, but as production increased, workers were brought into the area and a whole new town was built to house them. Not only did Arkwright provide living accommodation, he also constructed a chapel, a hotel and a school, as he insisted that all children working at his mill must be able to read and write.

This was in sharp contrast to other mill owners who exploited child labour and had a high mortality rate that is reflected in the number of ghost children reported. The only reported incident of a ghost child at Arkwright's mill happened a few years ago when the old machine shop was being converted into the shop in the yard. A member of staff at the time took a photograph of the area and when it was processed, there was the image of a ghostly little girl on the print.

Many years ago, the second, larger mill on the site was totally destroyed by fire and now only the blackened end wall still remains. Apparently a ghostly Victorian policeman tries to raise the alarm by banging frantically on the outside door of the block which now houses the exhibition centre. Many people have heard him and as recently as 1995, but one woman actually came face to face with him as she flung open the door. He was there for a second, then disappeared.

People have reported a feeling of oppression in the exhibition centre on the third floor of the first mill building. At one time, this was a laundry, but workers would not stay there alone. Lights are known to switch on and off on their own, but the strangest thing occurred about four years ago when a guide was escorting a family group round the mill. They were taking a keen interest and eventually they arrived at the exhibition room where one of them asked the guide something about Arkwright. Before he could answer, the father who later admitted to having psychic powers said, 'Ask him yourself. He's standing right next to you!'

Before 1770, Cromford was little more than a cluster of cottages around a packhorse bridge with a chapel where visitors prayed for a safe journey, but with Arkwright's arrival, Cromford became a self-sufficient community. As such, it has its fair share of ghosts and the village ghost walk is highly recommended. Just as an appetiser, here is one of the stories that relates to the village lock-up.

Used mainly for detaining drunks and nuisances, it was a rare occurrence when John Thompson was incarcerated there for four weeks after stealing a bale of cotton from Arkwright's mill. He was then transported to Australia, but apparently came back in body and in spirit. His ghost is said to haunt the lock-up where orbs and cold spots have been experienced by many visitors.

One hardy soul decided to raise money for charity by staying overnight in the lock-up, but he had to call it off in the middle of the night. Apparently he had been thoroughly spooked by the face of an old gaoler peering through the bars at him.

ILAM

The most breathtaking view of the picturesque border village of Ilam is from the open, twisting road to Blore. A natural starting point for exploring the valley, Ilam is where the remarkable River Manifold regains its overground course after its four-mile, subterranean journey through an underground lake.

A hall has stood at Ilam since John Port built the first one in 1546, but in 1820, the estate was bought by Jesse Russell, who made a fortune as a soap manufacturer when washing was becoming fashionable. He gave the whole estate to his eldest son, Jesse Russell Jr. who married Mary Watts, sole heiress to David Pike Watts. When he died in 1816, Jesse and Mary took the additional name of Watts, and it is Mary who commissioned the magnificent memorial to her father, seen in Ilam church.

Ilam Hall, with the haunted church to the right of the picture.

Mary and Jesse Watts-Russell made Ilam their principle country home and radically changed its appearance by demolishing the old hall and building their new home in baronial splendour. Because the valley and surrounding hills reminded them of the Alps, they were also responsible for the Swiss look, which is such a feature of Ilam scenery. After producing eight children, Mary died at the early age of 48 and, in her memory, Jesse commissioned the Gothic cross that stands in the centre of the village.

The hall, still an imposing and stately structure, had a substantial part demolished when it was presented by Sir Robert McDougall to the National Trust to form a youth hostel in 1934.

So, is there any psychic activity in this delightful setting? Apparently the ghost of a white lady has been seen wandering through the corridors of the hall. Others say she wanders round the Italian gardens and on to the church, and footsteps and noises have been heard around the stable block at night. Could this be Mary revisiting the home she loved?

*　　*　　*

A story told to me by a member of the National Trust staff involves a resident of Ilam who does not wish to be identified, so we will call him Joe. One evening, Joe left his comfortable fireside to lock the church. It was only a short distance from his home, but it was cold and dark and not the kind of night for loitering. Before locking the church door, he did a cursory check of the inside, sweeping his torch round the empty church, yet it was not empty. Sitting at the organ was a ghostly figure and ethereal music filled the church. Without stopping to investigate further, Joe turned and ran.

It is said that a phantom coach and horses turns round in the courtyard of Ilam Hall, possibly the same coach that is seen on the road to the ruined Throwley Hall. In the daytime, only the sound of its wheels can be heard, but at night its lights are seen. This particular coach has been given the name Cromwell Coach because of its connection to Robert Meverell of Throwley Hall whose memorial is in the church. His daughter married Thomas, Lord Cromwell.

Throwley Hall.

Throwley Hall is a 16th century manor house standing on an isolated spur overlooking the Manifold Valley. Three hundred years ago, Throwley Hall was a great house, but the roof was removed around 1910 and the structure has been open to the wind and rain since.

On the western side of the house stood a chapel from where a headless lady reportedly appears. There is also the spectre of a golden-haired little boy. He asks for directions home, but when asked where he lives, the boy points towards Throwley Hall, starts to sob then promptly disappears.

But watch out also for a phantom white horse with a headless rider said to gallop through the Manifold Valley on moonlit nights. It is alleged to be the ghost of a pedlar, murdered by two men who cut off his head and set his headless body back on his horse.

HANGING BRIDGE

anging Bridge is on the Derbyshire/Staffordshire border. Names like Hanging Bridge and Gallows Tree Lane, which drops down to the bridge, will always act as a reminder of the area's gruesome past. In 1745, when Bonnie Prince Charlie made his futile attempt to regain the crown for his father, many of his Jacobite soldiers and supporters were captured by the English and executed in this area. Apparently some still linger there.

In 1962, the actress Diana Dors stayed at a 16th century cottage in the area and had an experience that made headlines. Rumour has it that one night, she was woken from her sleep to find the apparition of a man standing by her bed. Although terrified, she was later able to describe him as having long, flowing hair and looking old and haggard. She was informed that she had probably seen the ghost of a Jacobite soldier and supporter of Bonnie Prince Charlie.

Locals believe Hanging Bridge is a place where evil spirits meet and it has certainly had its fair share of accidents and ghostly sightings, including a headless man and a ghost who is seen leaping off the bridge.

ASHBOURNE

ositioned on the gateposts of Ashbourne's historic church of St Oswald are huge pyramids resting on stone skulls. Some people might view them as decorative, but is there something more sinister in their use? Heads were revered by our Celtic ancestors because a person's spirit was believed to be held in the head. By lopping off their enemy's head it was believed they had not only defeated him, they would also possess his spirit. On Halloween or Shaim Armein, the spirits became free. So, to entice them back, a lighted taper or candle was put into the skull. This is the derivation of the Halloween pumpkin, hollowed out and cut to represent a skull with a candle burning inside.

The origin of the famous Royal Shovetide football game that takes place at Ashbourne every year is lost in time, but it is a held belief that the original ball

The decorative stone skulls at Ashbourne church.

was the head of a defeated enemy. It's now made of leather, filled with cork shavings and weighs 1.60 kg.

The churchyard of St Oswald is said to be the haunt of three haggard-looking ghosts, dressed in sackcloth and thought to have been victims of the plague. A ghost child is also seen regularly wandering around the gravestones and standing close to the main gate of the churchyard. She is believed to be Penelope Boothby who died in 1791, aged six. Her magnificent tomb inside Ashbourne church depicts this beautiful child in slumber.

Penelope Boothby.

*   *   *

If you leave Ashbourne on Spend Lane, the road to Fenny Bentley, take care! So many incidents have happened there, it is considered an accident black-spot, although many believe the lane is haunted.

In 1955, a car carrying a party of wedding guests crashed into a ditch on Spend Lane just at the same time as the top tier fell off the wedding cake at the reception.

In November 1977, a man was driving his car along Spend Lane, when it was suddenly filled with a tremendous wind, even though all the windows were tightly closed. There was the sound of upholstery ripping although the only damage found was a metal disc that had been torn off the dashboard.

In another incident on the lane, a girl was thrown by a normally well-behaved horse.

So what links these three incidents? It is widely believed that they are all connected with the tragic story of a bride killed on her wedding day. Apparently, the bride was travelling along Spend Lane from Fenny Bentley to her wedding in Ashbourne, but tragically, her carriage overturned and she was killed.

CARSINGTON

Another road leading out of Ashbourne passes through Carsington and it was on this road that a cyclist had a strange experience. It happened late one Saturday evening when he had finished milking at Ouslow Farm and was on his way home. It was dark, but his cycle was equipped with a carbide lamp which penetrated the darkness and illuminated the road and the verge either side, but as he reached Ouslow Hollow, he instinctively jammed on his brakes to avoid colliding with a woman who was crossing the road.

She seemed to pass through a thick thorn hedge, glide across the road and go straight through the opposite hedge. Trembling with disbelief, he mounted his bike and pedalled as fast as he could. Back home, he was able to describe the figure in accurate detail. She was middle-aged and wearing a dark, full-skirted dress with tight bodice, high collar and short cape. On her head was a close-fitting hat.

Later, after borrowing a book on period costume from the library, the man picked out a costume fashionable during the late Victorian and early Edwardian period. This dated the phantom lady to around 1900, but who she was remains a mystery.

SUDBURY

Sudbury Hall, east of Uttoxeter, is largely the creation of one man, George Vernon, who succeeded in 1660 and almost immediately began to rebuild the old manor house of his ancestors. Probably built to Vernon's own designs, this unusual Jacobean red brick building with patterned diapering has the most sumptuous interiors. With carvings by Grinling Gibbins, plasterwork by Bradbury and Pettifer, and painted ceilings by Louis Laguerre, it is not surprising that it was used in the filming of the BBC's *Pride and Prejudice*.

Sudbury Hall changed little until it was given to the Treasury in 1967 in part payment of duties after the death of the 9th Lord Vernon, and it was then transferred to the National Trust.

Two queens have lived in Derbyshire, one at Sudbury Hall, and although the stay of Mary, Queen of Scots is well documented, that of Queen Adelaide hardly gets a mention. This gentle, unpretentious lady was the wife of William IV who was the third, and most eccentric son of George III. William, created Duke of Clarence in 1789, had lived for 20 years with the actress Mrs Jordan. They had ten illegitimate children who took the name Fitzclarence, but when Mrs Jordan died, in 1818, William at the age of 53, married Adelaide of Saxe-Meiningen, a German princess who was half his age. Unfortunately, all her children died at birth or in infancy so when William succeeded George IV in 1830, they had no legitimate heir to the throne.

Adelaide had been queen for seven years when William died. His brother's daughter Victoria inherited, and the Queen Dowager chose to be independent.

Queen Adelaide's bedroom at Sudbury Hall.

After a spell in the Mediterranean, she moved to Derbyshire where in 1840, she rented Sudbury Hall from Lord Vernon who at the time was living in Italy. Despite her love for Sudbury, her health was never good and she returned to London where she died on 2nd December 1849.

However, it is believed that this quiet, compassionate queen still haunts the Great Staircase at Sudbury Hall, one of the finest of its kind in any English house. She is said to be dressed in black and looking ashen as she walks regally down the staircase, hesitates at the bottom step, then vanishes.

A lady in green who has been seen by workers and visitors also haunts the upper chambers of the house. The last reported sighting was in 1984 when two visitors saw a lady dressed in an old-fashioned green velvet dress pass them on their way to the Little Dining Room. Thinking it unusual they told one of the room-stewards who informed them they had seen the ghost of the 'Green Lady'.

A previous live-in worker woke one night to see the ghost of a maid watching her baby daughter, and another bedroom is said to be the haunt of a small girl who was burnt to death in a tragic accident.

KEDLESTON HALL

In the late 18th century, many grand houses were inspired by the designs of ancient Greece or Rome. This was known as the neo-classical style and Kedleston Hall, near Derby, designed by Robert Adam, and built for the Curzon family between 1759–1765, is one of the finest examples in the country.

According to staff, Kedleston Hall is almost devoid of spirits, though there has been the odd occasion when footsteps have been heard in the upper region of the house, doors have closed by themselves and staff have reported feeling

The haunting figure of Thomas Chatterton

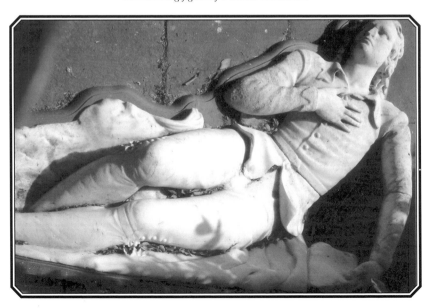

the hair on the back of their necks bristling. People have reported being spoken to by an unseen presence, and in the saloon, the custodian heard the sound of heavy breathing when no one but he was in there. The east wing where the family still live is said to be haunted by a poltergeist, resulting in things being moved, thrown and temporarily lost.

There is a strong suspicion that these phenomena could be caused by the ghost of Mrs Garnett, the housekeeper, who from 1766–1809 would show visitors round, and took a great pride in the hall.

Surprisingly, a female worker stated that late one evening and again on a foggy day, she watched from an upstairs window as a pale, ghostly and unhappy-looking figure walked in the gardens. It was believed to be the ghost of Thomas Chatterton (1752–70), an English poet and author of spurious medieval verse and prose. His recumbent statue was brought to the hall by Lady Ottilie, second wife of Richard, 2nd Viscount Scarsdale, and now lies in a passageway at the hall.

So what is his connection with Kedleston and why should he be there? Archivist Jill Banks could give no reason, but she did assure me that whatever spirits may be resident at Kedleston, they are all benign.

REPTON

Repton is the most historic and picturesque spot in south Derbyshire, and known for its famous school, so it is rather fitting to find a schoolboy ghost in the ancient building.

Apparently in 1853, Frederick Wickham-Railton, aged 14 years 8 months, in a form of initiation ceremony, was forced to run up and down the gallery while the boys lashed out at him with wet towels and pillowcases. But one boy had tied an inkbottle into the corner of his pillowcase and as the bottle hit Frederick violently on the head, he collapsed and died instantly. From that day on, the ghost of Frederick Wickham-Railton came back from the grave to haunt the school and his ghost is heard running up and down the gallery late at night.

Anchor church.

St Wystan church next to the school is the haunt of many ghosts. The 14th century tower and recessed spire harbours the mischievous spirit of a goblin who appears when there is a full moon. If caught, he will grant mortals one wish, provided it is made there and then, and the wish does not benefit the person.

The Saxon crypt is believed to have held the body of St Wystan. It is also the haunt of a hooded, monk-type figure, a humming ghost and a more demonic figure bathed in wreaths of smoke, who has also been seen sitting on a gravestone in the churchyard.

A 17th century gravedigger is also reported to haunt the area around the church. At one time, he would stand amongst the trees at the edge of the graveyard and watch the village gravedigger as he worked.

Pupils from the school that overlooks part of the churchyard have seen ghosts wander between the graves then mysteriously disappear. Could they vanish into the tunnel that according to legend runs from the graveyard to Anchor church, an impressive cave structure said to be haunted by at least one monk?

Unable to go by tunnel, we took the road to Foremark and Ingleby, then walked beside the river to find Anchor church, but what started as a gentle stroll turned into a one-mile hike, decidedly not to be undertaken by the faint hearted or anyone suffering from vertigo. With just the faint whisper of the river and intermittent birdsong, it's an incredibly beautiful but lonely area with a feeling of great calm. I tried not to think about the long history of hauntings that are associated with this stretch of the river, and the fishermen's stories of hearing ghostly fighting and crying.

Eventually we arrived at the area known as Black Pool where the beetling rocks are perforated with holes indicative of doors and windows. Scrambling up inside, the suggestion of a cave dwelling is even more obvious. Pillars of rock divide up the internal space to form rooms and all have panoramic views along the river. This is Anchor church, where a feeling of calm emanates from the walls and the floor bears indentations associated with the signs of kneeling for daily worship. It is also the abode of many unsettled souls, including a hermit, a wandering monk and a lady in white who glides along the riverbank. It is possible that this pure, young lady was sacrificed to the river gods, and then, compelled by Druidical magic, she protects the place she gave her life for.

•South-east Derbyshire•

DETHICK

Place names like Killburn and Killcroft must have been born out of some sinister circumstances in the past, but one name we can be sure of is Dethick, which literally means 'death oak'. This would indicate the site of a gallows or gibbet and, lying at the side of the road at a junction about one mile north-east of Dethick church, is a round, flat stone resembling a mill-stone but with a square hole cut in its centre. This is believed to have acted as the socket for the gibbet post, and locals still refer to it as the gibbet stone. Unsurprisingly, the area also has a history of hauntings.

But what gives Dethick its notoriety is its connection with the Babington family and the failed attempt by Anthony Babington to instate Mary, Queen of Scots as the rightful queen of England.

The Babingtons had strong Derbyshire connections and were actively involved in lead mining in the area. They owned a relatively modest country house at Dethick and Babington Hall, a town house that was demolished in 1826, in the centre of Derby. It stood opposite the Babington Buildings on the corner of Babington Lane, where on the gable is carved the family crest, a baboon on a tun or barrel.

Anthony Babington was born at Dethick in 1561 and, at the age of ten, was made a ward of George Talbot, the 6th Earl of Shrewsbury and his second wife, Bess of Hardwick, who in 1569 were given custody of Mary, Queen of Scots. Anthony Babington became a page to the 26-year-old Scottish queen and grew infatuated with her. Like all Catholics, Anthony considered Henry VIII's marriage to Anne Boleyn invalid and their daughter Elizabeth illegitimate,

Manor Farm, Dethick, the haunt of Anthony Babington.

whereas Mary, as the great-granddaughter of Henry VII should be the rightful queen of England.

With the help of John Ballard, a Catholic priest from Rheims and five others, Anthony Babington planned to murder Queen Elizabeth and put Mary on the throne. Part of the escape plan was for Mary to leave South Wingfield Manor where she was imprisoned, via a two-and-a-half mile tunnel to Manor Farm, his Dethick home. Unfortunately, Sir Frances Walsingham uncovered the plot and on 20th September 1585, the seven conspirators were taken to St Giles's in London where they were hung, drawn and quartered. Mary was executed seventeen months later on 8th February 1587 at Fotheringhay Castle. Her body was buried in Peterborough Cathedral, then moved to Westminster Abbey, but

South Wingfield Manor.

her spirit is said to wander aimlessly round the houses and castles in Derbyshire and Staffordshire in which she was imprisoned.

The lonely ghost of Anthony Babington is said to haunt Manor Farm, but for the romantics amongst us, there is a slightly happier ending. Legend says that Anthony used to visit Mary at South Wingfield Manor disguised as a gypsy, having dyed his skin with the oil from walnuts. A walnut dropped by

Anthony is said to have grown into the fully formed tree that is in front of Mary's apartments and the ghosts of Mary and Anthony have been seen together, sitting under that tree.

Wingfield was originally Winfield and probably derived its name from the quantity of win or gorse that grew wild in the locality. There is no record of a house until Wingfield Manor was built by Sir Ralph Cromwell, and 200 years later, razed by order of Oliver Cromwell. In that period it was little known until its then owner, the Earl of Shrewsbury, was made gaoler of Mary, Queen of Scots.

Of all the spiritual energies that have been felt and seen by visitors at Wingfield Manor, the most prolific is that of the unhappy queen. Her ghostly figure has been seen flitting around the ruins, and walking across the crypt where she disappears through a blocked doorway. Several people have heard sounds similar to footsteps, and a gardener has often smelt the scent of perfume around the entrance to the undercroft even though no one was around.

Workmen have seen lights in unoccupied areas and visitors have reported seeing a bluish light of indefinite shape in the undercroft, but these have all been individual incidents involving one or two spirits. Two workmen had just finished working in the crypt and taken their tools and equipment back to their van when one of the men realised he had left something behind. Returning alone to the crypt he encountered a full army of Parliamentary soldiers about to re-enact the destruction of the building.

LEA

Lea's most famous resident is undoubtedly Florence Nightingale, the 'Lady with the Lamp', who brought nursing out of the dark ages and made it a serious and respected profession.

Her wealthy family lived at Lea Hurst, yet even at an early age, Florence felt that her own affluence seemed wrong compared to the poverty and suffering of others. She spent her time distributing food and medicine to the sick who at that time were nursed at home. Only those with no relatives went into hospital, and few came out again.

Against her family's wishes, Florence was determined to gain valuable nursing experience and with the outbreak of the Crimean war, she took a small group of nurses over to Scutari barracks. There, she was able to improve conditions for thousands of soldiers who would have died through incompetence and disease rather than from their wounds. For the rest of her life, she continued to campaign for improvements in sanitation, public health and better conditions for British soldiers.

Many believe that Florence is still at Lea Hurst in spirit, and her ghost has been seen wandering along a top corridor and down the stairs. In 1940, the property passed from the Nightingale family to the Royal Surgical Aid Society (now known as AgeCare) and became a home for the elderly. Florence would have approved but sadly this closed in 2004 and the future of the building is at present in doubt. Whatever its future, Lea Hurst comes with the ghost of one of the greatest social reformers in history, firmly attached.

ALFRETON

Alfreton House is an attractive 17th century building on Alfreton High Street. It was built as the Gate Inn, later became the family home of the Rickard family and in the 20th century, the property of Derbyshire County Council. It has had many uses, but during the 1970s, part of the building was leased to the WRVS and used as a clothing depot.

Members of the WRVS, while sorting and stacking clothing, often experienced phantom footsteps and strange vibrations, and no one would stay in the building alone. Even more surprising, according to Mrs Joan Shacklock, the neatly-piled baby clothing was regularly disturbed as if someone had sorted through it. As the door to the store-room was kept locked, and there was never any sign of tampering, it was impossible for anyone to gain access to do this. Could this be a pregnant ghost searching for clothing for her new baby?

Alfreton House.

PINXTON

Cutting through the hills and across the coalfields between Pinxton and Barlborough is the 14½ mile Derbyshire stretch of the M1 motorway. The 23rd August 1965 saw the start of this £12,000,000 contract that met problems right from the start; bad weather conditions, an investigation into some 800 magnetic anomalies in the soil formation, and major subsidence associated with an area riddled with mine shafts, many uncharted. But that was just the start. Within a decade of its opening, there had been many horrendous accidents and traffic police blamed drivers for travelling too close, too fast and without due care and attention.

In July 1971, the *Derbyshire Times* was reporting on the problems caused by cloud-like emissions that hung over the motorway from the Coalite Plant at Bolsover, plunging drivers into thick murkiness. But that would not account for the high accident record along the remaining 14½ mile stretch. Some problems may be exacerbated by the design of the road, but people began to report strange phenomena and the motorway became directly associated in the popular imagination with hauntings.

In March 1978, the *Derbyshire Times* ran the story that a stretch of the M1 at Pinxton had more than its fair share of accidents. This section is often fog bound when no other is, claimed the paper, but is this a natural fog? Suggestions have been made that the motorway crosses the direct path where a ghost is alleged to walk, so if you are driving along this stretch, watch out for ghosts crossing!

DUFFIELD

Phantom coaches pulled by headless, black horses are encountered all over Derbyshire but the Duffield coach is an exception. This nightmarish apparition is a coach pulled by five white horses, with fiery eyes and smoking nostrils, being driven at a furious pace along the Valley of the Derwent. Manned by a skeleton coachman and postilions with grotesque features, as it approaches Duffield Bridge, it dashes into the river and disappears.

Phantom coaches are believed to be seen prior to a death in the family or unsurprisingly, anyone who gets in the way of a phantom coach will be carried away to their own doom!

MAKENEY

The archetypal highwayman was born in the aftermath of the Civil War when many Royalist officers were left without any means of support. Although terrorising travellers, the highwayman was portrayed as a romantic figure attired in fancy clothes, an aristocrat amongst thieves, who just happened to be down on his luck. That's the romantic image and the mystique that surrounds the highwayman owes much to this supposedly dashing young gentleman who would steal nothing from a pretty maid but a kiss. With a reputation greatly enhanced by his gallantry to ladies, his illicit affairs and his numerous narrow escapes, the highwayman soon became a popular folk hero, but by far the most famous was Dick Turpin.

Since he travelled through the area on a regular basis, the old Derby to Chesterfield road is steeped in Turpin folklore. Inns were an integral part of his life on the road, and as many old inns still exist, it is not surprising that several along this route claim, rather posthumously, to have enjoyed his custom.

In Makeney, at the 300-year-old Holly Bush Inn, a newspaper

Newspaper cutting requesting the return of Dick Turpin to Derbyshire.

cutting is displayed, asking for his body to be returned to Derbyshire. According to the 1890 Ward's Almanac, Dick Turpin was born in Horsley in 1705.

It is viable, as there are many Turpins living in the area and even more in the graveyard. Dick is reported to have stayed in a cottage next to Horsley church and at a farmhouse opposite the Coach and Horses Inn, but it is not possible to find a direct family link.

Dick is said to have been active around the Kilburn toll bar and reputedly a favourite lurking place for the highwayman was the incline up to Heage Common known as Dunge Hill, where it would have been comparatively easy to hold up a coach as it struggled up the hill.

Dating back to the 11th century, the Peacock Inn at Oakerthorpe was a major coaching inn, standing at the junction of what were three turnpike roads. Here until the 1950s, when it mysteriously disappeared, was a flintlock pistol reputedly dropped by Turpin while making an escape astride his faithful horse Black Bess.

At Higham, Dick stayed at what was then the Bull Inn, a coaching inn, later to become a farm. Now the barn where he slept has been made into two cottages named Turpin Cottages and the main road is known by the locals as Turpin Lane.

Dick Turpin was hung at York on 7th April 1739, but the ghost of the intrepid Dick has purportedly been seen at all the above. He has also been spotted astride a galloping Black Bess on The Chevin near Belper, standing at the crossroads on the old Belper to Ashbourne road, outside the Holly Bush Inn at Makeney and sitting in a tree at Duffield.

The Holly Bush Inn.

ELVASTON

People visit Elvaston Castle to admire the magnificent gardens and the Golden Gates that reputedly came from the Palace of Versailles, but the castle is currently not open to the public. The present building dates from the early nineteenth century and the time of the Gothic Revival, but a small part of the earlier brick-built manor house, home to the Stanhopes for 200 years, remains at the right of the south front. Here a mullioned windowed section bears the date 1633, and it is at one of these windows that the ghostly figure of a lady in white is seen moving from side to side as if sitting in a rocking chair. Could this be the beautiful Maria Foote, a celebrated actress, mistress of several Regency dandies and finally the Countess of Harrington?

In 1742 William Stanhope was created Earl of Harrington and Viscount Petersham. Almost 100 years on, the love affair of 'Beau' Petersham, later the 4th Earl of Harrington, and an actress was the talk of fashionable London, but after they married in 1831, she was kept a recluse at Elvaston Castle.

Elvaston Castle showing the earlier section where a ghost is seen at a window.

Maria Foote, Countess of Harrington.

For 20 years in this lonely, make-believe world, she must have longed for company and acclaim, and there are stories of her many eccentricities.

But is she still living here in her own private world? Does she roam from room to room, slamming doors and irritating people in the castle? Someone does!

According to staff in the gift shop, they often hear bumps and footsteps in the outbuildings that house the shop although they are empty, and sometimes they feel a presence so strongly that the hairs on the back of their necks stand on end.

The trim ghostly figure of a lady in white, accompanied by a large, white, spectral dog has also been seen in the grounds of the castle and going from the house to the nearby churchyard. There, she wanders around looking at gravestones and muttering to herself, perhaps rehearsing her lines from the days when she had a glittering career at Covent Garden.

SHARDLOW

Originally a river port, Shardlow developed significantly with the opening of the Trent and Mersey Canal in 1770, becoming an important centre where goods were transferred from the wide riverboats to the canal's narrow boats. Then the decline of the canal business

A busy scene outside the Malt Shovel, haunted by several ghosts.

threatened the area with dereliction, and the associated wharfs and warehouses fell into decline. Fortunately in 1975, conservation work was carried out and although the area is remarkably unchanged, it has been given a new lease of life. Shardlow's history is now on display at the Shardlow Heritage Centre and it has been placed second in the best-kept village competition several times.

Once, Shardlow might also have been placed in the top three in the most haunted village category, and I'm assured that the ghosts are still active. Only recently, a lady living opposite the old ropery saw a ghost flit across the road and disappear.

In the 1890s, a Shardlow lady encountered a strange man wearing immaculate evening dress but without a head, in her entrance hall. The lady told the story to her local vicar who recorded it with the comment – 'I am convinced of her sincerity'. Another headless man and a man dressed in the uniform of a Cavalier were seen some 50 years later.

The Lady in Grey restaurant, originally called The Lodge and the home of the Soarsby family, was renamed as an advertising gimmick, because a lady in grey supposedly haunts the house. She is believed to be Jeanette Soarsby who is still searching for the jewels given to her by her mother and hidden by her jealous sister who died before disclosing their whereabouts. Even in death, Jeanette refuses to give up her search, and many previous occupants and staff have seen this apparition dressed in a long, grey dress, wandering through the house and garden, and sitting on the balcony.

Now known as the Thai Kitchen Restaurant with an atmosphere evocative of Thailand, a less sympathetic background for the ghost of a Victorian lady would be hard to find. The owner Gung assured me he had no personal experience of the ghost of the Grey Lady, but his mother and several of his staff have felt her presence and that of a young boy.

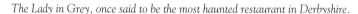

The Lady in Grey, once said to be the most haunted restaurant in Derbyshire.

At one time in Shardlow, for a population of 650, there were thirteen pubs and three breweries all brewing their own beer and extracting malt by boiling barley. In 1799, Humphrey Moore, a rich farmer, owned one brewery and was responsible for the building of the malt house where an unknown worker fell into a boiling vat and died a horrible death. The malt house is now the Malt Shovel pub, and this poor wraith is said to haunt the cellars, according to Peter Hanson, an ex-landlord who saw him quite recently.

Another casualty of drink walked straight into the canal and drowned. His body wasn't found until the next day, and his spirit haunts the canal side. A third presence is believed to be a one-legged beggar who was murdered in one of the old buildings hereabouts.

At the Old Salt Warehouse, one of the oldest buildings in Shardlow and a warehouse for the river trade prior to the canal's construction, Pat and Jeff Clifton ran an antique business. Previous occupants reported poltergeist activity and at times Jeff felt his hair stand on end but never actually saw anything, although in one area it was often icy cold.

Jeff's family farmed at Ridings Hill, which stands on an island of higher ground within the flood plain between the Trent and Mersey Canal and the River Trent. The area was called Dead Man's Drop as the gibbet had stood there, and 80 yards away was a solitary oak tree. When gravel began to be dug out there, rumours started to circulate about the oak being a witch's tree, planted to contain the body of a witch within its roots, and protected by a curse on anyone who removed the tree. Five sturdy ash trees were torn out but no one was brave enough to touch the oak despite the loss of 11,000 tons of gravel.

With the construction of the A50, Tarmac moved in. They questioned the lone tree and soon the *Derby Telegraph* ran the story, but there was another mystery too. A cottage that had once been a communal milking barn was destroyed, and 40 yards away in the foundations of a second were found two skeletons with both their heads and hands cut off.

The area is now a peaceful lagoon and will be landscaped in the near future, so all trace of its macabre past will soon have been obliterated forever, but will this quieten the ghosts?

Press cuttings relating to the 'Witch's tree'.

MELBOURNE

Melbourne Castle might have changed English history but in September 1584, when the Privy Council wanted the Earl of Shrewsbury to take Mary, Queen of Scots there, it was in need of a few alterations. Instead, Mary was taken to South Wingfield Manor where Anthony Babington tried to plot her escape. How different things might have been if Melbourne had been a more desirable residence.

Melbourne Pond.

As it happened, it never did get those alterations. It was cannibalised and the stone, previously quarried from the area which is now the pond, was used to build Melbourne Hall. A corn mill which originally stood by this pond gave Melbourne its name; literally mill-bourne (the mill boundary).

Melbourne Hall became the seat of the Coke family. Around 1696, Sir Thomas Coke altered the house to the building we see today, but as he died without producing a son, his daughter Charlotte inherited with her husband Matthew Lamb. Their son, Sir Peniston Lamb, was created the first Viscount Melbourne, a title that passed to his second son William, Queen Victoria's first Prime Minister. When Queen Victoria gave her name to the Australian state, she named the capital after her Prime Minister, Lord Melbourne, who had taken his title from this Derbyshire village.

Prime Minister William fell in love with the beautiful Caroline Ponsonby. They married, but Lady Caroline Lamb (as she then became) was quite a

The Birdcage, haunt of Lady Caroline Lamb.

notorious lady, having scandalous and very public affairs with people like Lord Byron from nearby Newstead Abbey.

Unfortunately, Lady Caroline suffered from severe mental illness and died in 1828. Now her ghost is said to be grounded at Melbourne Hall, wandering around the beautiful gardens to vanish into the unique arbour, known as the Birdcage.

CALKE

The faded splendour of Calke Abbey provides a unique insight into a fine Baroque house which stands on the site, and incorporates some of the fabric of a medieval religious house of the Augustinian canons. Secularised in the reign of Henry VIII, any traces of earlier masonry have been disguised by rebuilding in 1701 and 1841, and apart from minor repairs and improvements in 1865, the introduction of the telephone in 1928 and electricity in 1962, this is the house where time has stood still.

When the house passed to the National Trust in 1985 it was in need of extensive repairs, but Calke Abbey was also ready to reveal many treasures and secrets. Excavating for drains and electricity cables on the east side of the house exposed not only the remains of the priory buildings, but five adult male skeletons dating from the 12th to 14th centuries. They were laid along a strict east/west axis which suggests they were the remains of the monastic occupants of Calke Priory, and although they are now buried in consecrated ground, do their ghosts remain at Calke?

Various members of the public have seen a hooded monk in the toilet block. In the Old Brewhouse, a steward heard footsteps race along the servants' passage and gallop up the stone stairs. The family who emerged were all in shock. They had been walking along the servants' passage following an elderly man in what they thought was a long flowing coat, when he simply vanished before their eyes.

In the Chop House, where animal feed was prepared and which is now the information and ticket office, staff have experienced being pinched and

Calke Abbey, haunt of an Augustinian monk, Lady Caroline Harpur and Nanny Pearce.

slapped, and on several occasions the wooden chairs used by visitors have been found on the table.

A steward saw a figure glide through the ground floor lobby, a part of the surviving 1701 entrance to the eastern wing, and one day, a normally well-behaved cat went berserk in there and has refused to enter since.

There are indications that in the 17th and 18th centuries, the living rooms were in the east wing, and until about 1860, the Boudoir, the Yellow Room and the Schoolroom on the first floor comprised one of the principle apartments of the house. They now appear to be the most spiritually active. Staff working in the rooms below have heard footsteps through these rooms, despite the fact no one was there.

In the first-floor library, which was created in 1805 and was formerly the drawing room, visitors have reported seeing an elderly lady sitting watching them. Her description tallies with that of Nanny Pearce, an old and trusted retainer who stayed on after the children had grown too old for her services.

One visitor saw a lady in period dress in the boudoir. He assumed it was an actor, especially as she looked exactly like the lady in the portrait hanging in that room. The portrait is of Lady Caroline, wife of Sir Henry Harpur, the 5th baronet. It wasn't until later when he was assured that no actors were circulating that day, that he realised he had seen a ghost.

In the Yellow Room, the Property Manager has felt a strange pressure build up, and in the schoolroom next door, while closing the shutters, he felt a hand on his shoulder. Could it be Nanny Pearce, a troubled monk or Lady Caroline, three spirit entities who have all showed themselves so vividly?

· Bibliography ·

Telling people that I was researching for a book on Derbyshire ghosts often brought the response – 'Not another book.' At one time I might have said the same thing as some excellent books have been written on the subject. However, many are now out of print, places change, people are more willing to divulge their spectral secrets and new stories come to light. I feel that I've only skimmed the surface, but I hope I've mentioned most of the Derbyshire places that have been, at some time in the past, said to be haunted, updated them with fresh findings and discovered some great, new stories.

As space is at a premium, here is a list that will further your interest and give you more great reading. Enjoy.

Murder & Mayhem in the Peak, Roly Smith, Halsgrove

Pub Strolls in the Peak District, Peter Fooks, Countryside Books

Haunted Derbyshire, Clarence Daniels, Dalesman

Ghosts of Derbyshire, Clarence Daniels, Dalesman

Hanged for a sheep, E.G Power, Scathin Books

The Encyclopedia of Ghosts & Spirits, John & Anne Spencer, Headline

Ghosts of Derbyshire, Wayne Anthony, Breedon Books

Derbyshire Ghosts & Legends, David Bell, Countryside Books

Ghosts of Chesterfield, R.A Pearson

Ghosts of Derby, Wayne Anthony & Richard Felix, Breedon Books

Supernatural Peak District, David Clarke (*Sheffield Star* and *Derby Telegraph*), Robert Hale

Derbyshire Times various articles

•Index•